HUMAN RIGHTS

HUMAN RIGHTS

Adil-Ul-Yasin

Archana Upadhyay

AKANSHA PUBLISHING HOUSE

NEW DELHI-110 059 (INDIA)

AKANSHA PUBLISHING HOUSE
4649-B/21, Ansari Road
Daryaganj, New Delhi-110002
Phones: 011-23263193, 09435116718
Email: ektabooks@yahoo.com
visit us: www.akanshapublishinghouse.com

Human Rights

First Edition **2004**
Reprint **2018**
Reprint **2020**

PRINTED IN INDIA

Published by Akansha Publishing House, New Delhi-110002.

For our cherished friend and
valued colleague,
A.N.S. AHMED,
to whom we owe so much

PREFACE

The concept of "Human rights" is as ancient as human civilization. The history of mankind is marked by efforts to ensure respect for the dignity of human beings. Human Rights are simply defined as the rights which every human being is entitled to enjoy and to have protected. The struggle for the recognition of human rights and the struggle against political, economic, social and cultural oppression, against injustice and inequalities, have been an integral part of the history of all human societies.

The roots of the contemporary conception of human rights can be traced to the period of *Renaissance* and *Enlightenment*. This period was characterized by a system of views called humanism, which extolled man, stressed his essential worth and dignity, expressed deep faith in his limitless creative potential, and proclaimed freedom of the individual and inalienable rights of the individual.

The last quarter of the eighteenth century witnessed the emergence of revolutionary movements challenging the despotic and authoritarian political regimes of the time. The movements made the rights of man the fundamental basis of their struggle as well as of the new order that they sought to build. The two most important declarations which inspired revolutionary movements the world over were the *American Declaration of Independence* (1776) and the *French Declaration of the Rights of Man and Citizen* (1789). These declarations most certainly had a universal character. In the nineteenth century, the socialist movement with its stress on the '*abolition of class rule*' and the establishment of social and economic equality, provided a new thrust to the evolving concept of human rights.

While the roots of the contemporary conception of human rights and its universal nature is based on the rich heritage of the past, it is imperative that it is seen and understood in the specific historical context of the twentieth century. The first half of the twentieth century was characterized not only by the prevalence of colonial rule in large parts of the world but also the rise of authoritarian governments and the establishment of Fascist and aggressive regimes in some countries of the world. The period also witnessed the rise of national liberation movements and of movements for democracy and social progress in different parts of the world. The twentieth century also saw the two most devastating wars in human history - the First World War and the Second World War. The period between the two World Wars have been very aptly described as the *Age of Catastrophe*. In was in the closing years of this period, which also witnessed the war against fascism that the conceptualization and articulation of human rights in its present form took place. The most significant feature of the new conceptualization was its universality. It was expressed in the Charter of the United Nations (1945) which began with the following words: "*We the Peoples of The United Nations Determined* to save succeeding generations from the scourge of war which twice in our life time has brought untold sorrow to mankind, and to reaffirm faith in fundamental human rights, in the dignity and worth of the human person, in the equal rights of men and women and of nations large and small, and to establish conditions under which justice and respect for the obligations arising from treaties and other sources of international law can be maintained, and to promote social progress and better standards of life in larger freedom...." The Universal Declaration of Human Rights proclaimed in 1948 is the contemporary statement of human rights which are intended to be universally applicable. Although the Universal Declaration of Human Rights is simply a statement of intent or principle without any legal binding, it has influenced the constitutions and legal systems of many countries. The Universal Declaration has been followed by many covenants/conventions which present in an elaborate form the human rights principles in respect of specific issues and aspects. These covenants/conventions are very important as the countries that are signatories to them have explicitly agreed to follow them.

The evolution of the contemporary concept of human rights is commonly understood in terms of three generations of human rights. The *first generation rights* were concerned mainly with the civil and political rights of the individual. These rights were meant to impose 'negative obligations on governments to desist from interfering with the exercise of individual liberties'. These rights were among the major concerns of all liberal and democratic movements since the nineteenth century.

The *second generation rights* provide for social, economic and cultural security. These rights are more positive in nature in that they make it the duty of the state to ensure that these rights are realized. The Universal Declaration of Human Rights reflects the consensus on the principles which form the basis of the first and second generation rights.

The *third generation of human rights* are of relatively recent origin. They have evolved in response to various new concerns over which international consensus has emerged in recent years. These include environmental, cultural and developmental rights. They are concerned with rights of groups and peoples rather than of individuals and include such rights as the right to self-determination and the right to development. The Declaration on the Right to Development adopted by the UN General Assembly in 1986 is the most important example of these rights.

Ever since the adoption of the Universal Declaration, there have been many controversies regarding the question of the importance of civil and political rights over economic, social and cultural rights and vice-versa. These controversies have been resolved by the *Vienna Declaration* (1993) which recognized the indivisible nature of all human rights. The Vienna Declaration, issued after a conference in which representatives of 171 countries and hundreds of non-governmental organizations participated, unambiguously affirmed that "All human rights are universal, indivisible, interdependent and interrelated". It has also been affirmed that democracy is the sole guarantor of individual rights - civil, political, economic, social and cultural - and collective rights 'within states and within the community of states'.

As already stated, the Universal Declaration has influenced the constitution and legal systems of various countries. Many countries are signatories to the covenants/conventions on human rights which implies that they have undertaken to implement them. The declarations, though statements of intent or principle, are equally applicable. Therefore, it is the responsibility of the governments to protect and promote all these rights. However, it is necessary to remember the distinction between human rights as articulated in international declarations and covenants/ conventions and rights that are laid down in the law of the country and can be enforced, if necessary, through the intervention of the courts.

Indisputable achievements in codification and the progressive development of international human rights law have not met with equal success in the observance of the latter. Regrettably human rights are violated everyday in many parts of the world. Progress in their implementation depends on a number of factors, among which knowledge of relevant standards and procedures is not the least; it is obvious that human rights and fundamental freedoms can only be observed when they are known. Education for human rights is therefore of great importance. This has been recognized in many international instruments. Article 26 of the Universal Declaration of Human Rights states that 'education shall be directed to the full development of human personality and to the strengthening of respect for human rights and fundamental freedoms'. Education in human rights has thus been viewed as an essential contribution to the development of a global human rights culture.

This compilation has been worked out with a view to making major human rights documents accessible to the large body of personnel involved in various sectors of education - policy formulation, curriculum development, classroom and out-of-class teaching - learning activities - to enrich the human rights education programme as the basis for promoting awareness of current issues and controversies relating to human rights.

We hope that the present compilation will be found useful by all those who are interested in promoting human rights and human rights education. We welcome readers' comments and suggestions on any aspect of this book.

Very often in a work of this nature, it is the people behind the scenes we make so much of the work possible. We would particularly like to acknowledge the contribution of our respective families. Their support and encouragement has been a constant source of inspiration for us.

Dibrugarh
7th October, 2003

ADIL-UL-YASIN
ARCHANA UPADHYAY

CONTENTS

Appendices

1

HUMAN RIGHTS: Definition and Evolution of the Concept

Meaning, Nature and Development

Human Rights are inherent and inalienable rights which are due to an individual by virtue of his/her being a human being. These rights are necessary to ensure the dignity of every person as a human being irrespective of one's race, religion, nationality, language, sex or any other factor. The concept of Human Rights are based on the assumption that human beings are born equal in dignity and rights. These are moral claims which are inalienable and inherent in all human individuals by virtue of their humanity alone. These claims are articulated and formulated in what is today understood as human rights. These rights have been translated into legal rights, established according to the law-creating processes of societies, both national and international. The basis of these legal rights is the consent of the governed.

The values of dignity and equality of all members of the human race, like many other basic principles which underlie what we today call human rights, can be found in virtually every culture and civilization, religion and philosophical tradition.[1] However, human life and human dignity have been disregarded throughout history and continue to be disregarded today. Discrimination continues to exist due to ignorance, prejudice and fallacious doctrines which try to justify inequality. Such doctrines have been used to defend discrimination on the grounds of sex, race, colour, descent, ethnic origin, religious belief or on the basis of class or caste systems, throughout history and unfortunately even in modern times. Human Rights are based on mankind's increasingly demand for a life in which the inherent dignity and worth of each human being will receive respect and protection. These rights enable individuals to fully use their intelligence, talents and conscience to satisfy their spiritual and other needs.

The ideas of elaboration and protection of rights of human beings have been gradually transformed into written norms. Many important landmarks may be mentioned on this way, such as, the *Magna Carta* in England (1215), the *American Declaration of Independence* (1776), the *French Declaration on the Rights of Man* (1789) and the *Bolshevik Revolution in Russia* (1917). Each of these declarations has made important contribution in advancing the concept of human rights. However, being products of their own time and specific circumstances, they were narrow in their scope and application. For instance, in the Greek political system, rights existed only for the "citizens" and not for the majority who were referred to as "slaves". Although the Magna Carta did set limitations to arbitrary rule and laid the foundation for the rule of law, the real beneficiaries of these concessions were the feudal lords and not the common man. The American Declaration followed by constitutional amendments or Bill of Rights contained fairly exhaustive guarantees for the rights of man; but in practice their application was largely confined to those who constituted the WASP (White, Anglo-Saxon and Protestant). Slavery continued to be a part of the system. It was in 1864 that slavery in America was legally abolished after a bitter civil war, which threatened the unity and integrity of the country itself.

By the end of the eighteenth century, in Europe and North America, the concept of natural right was secularized, rationalized and democratized. The concept of "the Rights of Man" emerged. This concept covered substantially what came to be known as civil and political rights. Towards the mid-nineteenth century, within the industrial-capitalistic economy of Europe and North America, trade union rights, better wages and better working conditions considerably improved the lot of the majority constituting the working class. Flow of wealth and additional resources from colonial territories also had a cumulative effect in ensuring, along with civil liberties, a minimum of economic and social security to almost all the people in North America and Europe. While countries in Europe and North America, were moving towards larger freedoms both political and economic, the people of the rest of the world continued to be victims of colonial and imperialist exploitation. During the colonial era, it was inevitable that rights available to the citizen's in metropolitan countries were denied by the same metropolitan powers to their "subject" people in the colonies. As a consequence, the interaction and comparison between peoples of the two sides helped generate wider awareness and demand for human rights among the peoples under colonial rule.

As a result of the convergence of several historical factors, in the middle of the twentieth century, a concept of human rights, universal in its approach and comprehensive in its content emerged. This development found expression in the Charter of the United Nations - the first international instrument which, in unequivocal terms proclaimed universal respect for, and observance of, human rights and fundamental freedom for all without distinction as to race, sex, language or religion. The UN Charter made promotion of these rights as one of its basic purposes and obligated member states to take joint and separate action in cooperation with the United Nations for the achievement of this purpose.

The human rights movement has progressed to a point where in its fundamental conception, it treats members of the human race as members of a global community and, therefore, broadly entitled to a common pattern of human rights. Some of the widely accepted definitions of Human Rights are as follows:

- The *United Nations Centre for Human Rights* defines Human Rights "as those rights which are inherent in our nature and without which we cannot live as human beings"[2].
- Human Rights have also been defined as moral rights of the higher order stemming from 'socially shared moral conceptions of the nature of the human person and the condition necessary for a life of dignity'.[3]
- For Kim, human rights represent 'claims and demands essential to the protection of human life and the enhancement of human dignity, and should therefore enjoy full social and political sanctions[4].'
- Nickel characterizes human rights as 'norms which are definite, high priority, universal and existing and valid independently of recognition or implementation in the customs or legal systems of particular countries'[5].
- For Falk, human rights are not merely legal or moral abstraction but they "are embedded in historical process ... closely intertwined

with the on-going anti-imperial struggle against political, economic and cultural structures of international domination"[6].

- Szabo puts human rights within the framework of constitutional law, the purpose of which is "to defend by institutional means the rights of human beings against abuses of power committed by the organs of the state and at the same time to promote the establishment of humane living conditions and the multi-dimensional development of human personality"[7].

It has been argued that the international concern for human rights as enshrined in the *Charter of the United Nations* is not a modern innovation. It is 'heir to all the great historic movements for man's freedom, to the enduring elements in the tradition of natural rights and in most of the world's great religions and philosophies and to the finding of contemporary science about the interrelations of simple respect for human dignity and other individuals and community values[8]. The term 'human rights' is used as a twentieth century version for what has traditionally been, known as 'natural rights of Man.'[9] 'Right of Man' was the slogan of the revolutionaries worldwide, especially in the 18th and 19th centuries and attempts were made to fix up the minimum rights that could be demanded by all the citizens by the very fact of being human from the governments that ruled them.[10] It was only after the First World War that international activity concerning human rights was given an institutional form. The League of Nations accepted in its Covenant the obligation to secure and maintain fair and humane conditions of labour for men, women and children. However, it was only after the establishment of the United Nations that human rights became one of the central preoccupations of international relations. The most important reason for the emergence of human rights as a matter of international concern is to be found in the broadened definition of peace which has found acceptance throughout the world. The UN Charter does not take a negative view of peace as 'absence of war', but is based on understanding that there is a symbiotic relation between the political-security aspect of peace and the human rights aspect of peace.

From the above definitions, the following characteristics of Human Rights become evident:

– It is a right of an individual or a group of individuals.

– These rights are inalienable and human beings are entitled to them by birth.

- It is a universal and legal concept.
- These rights are meant to uphold human dignity and equality and to set forth liberty and fraternity to all without any kind of discrimination.
- These rights are the basic minimum requirement for survival of human beings in Society.
- These rights can be executed only within the society and are protected and enforced by the authority of the state at all levels.

Three Generation Rights

It is common to refer to the evolving concept of human rights in terms of three generations of human rights:

i. The *first generation* of human rights are those which originated in Europe in the 18th Century. These rights emerged from the American and French revolutions. They were aimed at securing the citizen's liberty from arbitrary action by the state. These rights correspond by and large to the civil and political right in the International Bill of Rights such as the right to individual freedom, freedom of speech, thought and faith, the right to own property and so on. These rights were meant to impose 'negative obligations on governments to desist from interfering with the exercise of individual liberties'. These rights were among the major concerns of all liberal and democratic movements since the nineteenth century.

ii. The *second generation* of human rights emerged in the 19th century out of the political and economic struggles of the emergent working class and included political and economic demands like the right to participate in the exercise of political power, the right to universal adult franchise; the right to fixed hours of work; the right to minimum wages; the right to form unions and so on. These rights were conceptualized and legalized in the West in course of a series of agitation and struggles corresponding to the various stages of economic growth under a capitalist system. These rights are also said to be 'security-oriented' as it provides for social, economic and cultural security. These rights - social, economic and cultural - are more positive in nature in that they make it the duty of the state to ensure that these rights are realized. The Universal Declaration of Human Rights reflects the consensus on the principles which form the basis of the first and second generation rights.

iii. The *third generation* of human rights emerged in the twentieth century through the socio-political turmoil of the two World Wars. These rights are a response to the phenomenon of global interdependence. These rights are of relatively recent origin. They have evolved in response to various new concerns over which international consensus has emerged in recent years. These include environmental, cultural and developmental rights. They are concerned with the rights of groups and peoples rather than of individuals and include such rights as the right of self-determination and the right to development. The Declaration on the Right to Development adopted by the UN General Assembly in 1986 is the most important example of these rights.

Theories of Human Rights

Broadly speaking, the socio-political theories of Human Rights can be placed under two categories: *the Classical Liberal Theories* and the *Modern International Theories_of International Human Rights.*

Classical Liberal Theory of Human Rights

The genesis of the concept of human rights can be traced to the emergence of classical liberalism. Classical liberalism made a passionate defense of the principles like competitive individualism, private property and market ethics. It cherished the realization of individual's liberty, his development and human progress through the functioning of the above principles. The ideas of the rule of law, limited government and individualism characterized the seventeenth and eighteenth century school of political liberalism.

The *Liberal-Individualist-Theory of Natural Rights* is the earliest theory of rights. Though it can be traced back to the Greek times, yet it came to the fore in the seventeenth century when a persistent and powerful body of opinion in the West popularized the idea that all men possess certain rights by nature irrespective of particular political, social or legal institutions. The individual had some natural, inalienable, fundamental, inherent, absolute and sacred rights by birth. These rights were independent of society and the state. According to the exponents of the theory, natural rights are pre-political and, according to some they are also pre-social. Although this theory is the oldest theory of rights yet it gained distinct recognition from the authors of the *Social Contract Theory.* In practical politics it exerted great influence on the constitutional struggle of America and France.

Views of Hobbes, Locke and Rousseau

Thomas Hobbes

Thomas Hobbes (1588 - 1679) one of the greatest English political theorists, wrote his masterpiece the *Leviathan* in 1651. Hobbes, so frequently portrayed as the great absolutist, is perhaps the greatest individualist in the history of political thought. His doctrine is an extreme doctrine of individualism embracing everything. The individual who he describes in his *State of Nature* has the faculty of reasoning. Men in such a state are continually in competition for honour and dignity resulting in envy, hatred and finally war. Neither right nor wrong, justice nor injustice, have a place in such a state of nature. Force and fraud are its cardinal virtues, and the only rule that men acknowledge is that of *might is right.* Men, Hobbes believes, will do anything to get out of this desperate position. This is possible because men happen to be creatures of passion, imagination, reason and will. Reason teaches them to obey *Natural Laws,* which Hobbes describes as the 'doctrine of civil society'.[11] For Hobbes Natural Laws are "counsels of prudence"[12] Hobbe's Natural Laws do not imply that there is such a thing as a common good. They merely seek to bring into being those common conditions which are necessary to fulfil each individual good, Man, who is born free, solitary, and in intellectual and moral isolation, voluntarily accepts limitation of sovereignty to achieve something else. He composes a society by *human agreement,* an artifice. Hobbes believes that the third party, who is the beneficiary of the contract, the recipient of power, should be a King. Hobbe's doctrine is a doctrine of the absolute state, not of the absolute king. *The Law of Nature* can never be pleaded against the Leviathan, for the purpose of the Law of Nature is the creation of Leviathan, who alone can interpret it.

Although Hobbes makes the Leviathan all-powerful, he never forgets that it is something artificial. The State according to him is a machine, an artifact, a contrivance of man. It is the result of a contract which presupposes the consent of all the parties to it. If the Leviathan fails to protect, men are then back in the state of nature. The sole justification for the existence of the state is that it preserves the citizens. The moral authority of the state derives from the consent of the governed. Thus,

Hobbe's Leviathan is not merely a forceful enunciation of the doctrine of Sovereignty and of the machine view of the state, it is also a powerful statement of Individualism. Hobbes is the first modern thinker to view the state as the conciliator of interests. In this he is the forerunner of the Utilitarians.

John Locke

John Locke's (1632 - 1704), two very notable works are his *Essay Concerning Human Understanding* and his *Essays on Civil Government.* Next to Hobbes, Locke is the greatest figure in the history of English political thought. According to Locke, desire is the spring of all human action. Desire is a feeling of uneasiness identified with pain, a feeling of which men want to rid themselves. The object of all human action is to substitute pleasure for pain. Locke points out that the state of nature is a state in which men are equal and free to act as they think fit, within the bounds of the law of nature. From this *Natural Law* man derives certain natural rights, rights to life, liberty, and property. His right to liberty is his right to do whatever he wants so long as that is not incompatible with the Law of Nature. His right to property is his right to anything with which he has mixed his labour, provided he makes good use of it. However, Natural Law not only accords man rights, it also imposes duties upon him. This state of nature, in which men have rights and acknowledge duties, is moral and social in character. Nevertheless, it has its inconveniences. Although, it is not a state of war, it is a state in which peace is not secure. It leaves unsatisfied three important wants - the want of an "established, settled, known law", the want of a "known and indifferent judge", and the want of an executive power to enforce just decisions.[13]

To get out of the state of nature; according to Locke, men make a contract to enter into civil society. This is a contract of all with all. This is a social as well as political contract. It is a contract which, once made, is irrevocable. It is a contract to which each generation must consent. However, it is a contract in which men give up some and not all of the rights they possessed in the state of nature. The contract is no more than a surrender of certain rights and powers whereby man's remaining right will be protected and preserved. It is not general as with Hobbes but limited and specific. This contract does not, as with Hobbes, put an end to the Law of Nature as it does to the state of Nature. Man in the State continues to be under the law, as he was before. This contract, is the first step to the drawing up of a trust. People, having forned a society, must then institute a government.

For Locke, the form of the state is a secondary matter. It may be a democracy, an oligarchy, a hereditary or an elective monarchy. The first and most important characteristic of Locke's State is that it exists for the people who form it, they do not exist for it. Locke repeatedly insists that the end of the government is the good of the community. He further insists that all true states must be founded on consent and must be a constitutional state in which men acknowledge the rule of law. Government must therefore be by established standing laws, promulgated and known to the people, and not be extemporary decrees. The most important characteristic of Locke's true state is that it is limited and not absolute. It is limited by Natural Law. Civil Law for Locke is merely the restatement of Natural Law in detail and by authorized legislation. The particular Natural Law which limits the power of the state is that which gives men a right to their property. The right to property, Locke insists, is a natural right which is in existence before political institutions.

Three further characteristics of the good state remain to be noticed. It is a *tolerant state,* which will respect differences of opinion. It is a *negative state,* which does not seek to improve the character of its citizens nor to manage their lives, but which merely strives to secure their independence. The state is also a *transformer state,* transforming selfish interest into public good. Lock points out that the end of law is not to abolish or restrain, but to preserve and enlarge freedom. A state which is not constitutional and which exceeds its authority can be legitimately overthrown. Locke however, makes a distinction between the dissolution of the society and the dissolution of the government and points out that the latter does not entail the former.[14]

Locke's worth and importance remain beyond doubt. His is the last great voice of one great tradition and the first great voice of another great tradition. Locke's work is the very important continuation into the modern world of the great medieval tradition of political liberty. It is also the first striking formulation of the principles of the Liberal State, a very strong plea that the function of the government is to remove oppression and increase liberty. Locke laid down the essential theses of liberalism — that people are the source of all political power; that government cannot be justified unless it possesses their free consent, that all governmental measures are to be judged by an active citizen body; that men are reasonably moral and responsible and that the main object of government is to help them when they require it, but not to run their lives for them; and finally that the state must be resisted if it steps beyond its proper authority.

Jean Jacques Rousseau

Jean Jacques Rousseau (1712 - 1778) has been described both as an extreme individualist and an extreme absolutist. On the one hand he was a stern asserter of the state and on the other hand he was a fiery champion of the individual. In his *Discourse on the Origin and Foundation of Inequality,* Rousseau put forward his ideas on the nature of man. In his view, two original instincts made up man's nature. These were self-love or the instinct of self-preservation and sympathy or the gregarious instinct. In other words, man by nature is good. Rousseau points out that conscience and reason which are in close attendance on man together restrain the desire that is in him. Hence the "natural" man will be one in whom strong conscience and steadfast reason have successfully harmonized self-love and sympathy. Reason will seek not only to harmonize but also to develop man's instincts, to give them the fullest expression. For this, culture and society will be necessary. It is only within the society that man enjoys full freedom of action and enjoys true liberty.

It is in the *Social Contract* that Rousseau's idea of the state is most clearly seen. He starts with the belief that the family is the only "natural" society. All other society, according to him, is of man's making and artificial and rests on agreement. Men register their agreement to come together in society in the social contract. The social contract is not a contract which men make with their future ruler. The Government is merely their agent. To make a contract with it would not only give it a dignity to which it ought not to pretend, it would place men under the rule of some individuals or groups, which would be nothing but slavery. Such a contract would defeat the ends for which men come together. For men not only need society in which to develop; without freedom they cannot develop. Therefore their problem is to create a society in such a way that each, when united to his fellows, renders obedience to his own will and remains as free as he was before. According to Rousseau, this is possible where the law leads and men do not obey other men but obey only the law. It is to law alone that men owe justice and liberty. It is law alone that dictates to each citizen the precepts of public reason, and teaches him to act in accordance with the maxims of his own judgement and not to be in contradiction to himself. This law is the voice of the *General Will.*[15] General Will is thus the will of all the citizens when they are willing not their own private interest but the general good; it is the voice of all for the good of all. The General will is inalienable and indivisible besides being general in every sense. It must take account of the voice of every citizen, since it was agreed in the contract that each is received as an integral part of the group. It must bind all equally, since that also is implied in the contract in which each surrenders his all on equal terms. It must deal only with the generalities of legislation, with the common cause and not with private interests - though it alone will decide what is common cause and what are private interests. It is, in fact, only the fundamental laws that shape the constitution of the state that Rousseau regards as law, and therefore as the product of the General Will.

General Will, according to Rousseau, cannot be an executive will. The people ought not to be responsible for the details of Government. Those who make the law should not carry it out, for it is the characteristic of the Sovereign General Will that it must be impersonal. Rousseau makes a clear distinction between the Government and the Sovereign People. The People entrust its executive power to its agent, the government, though it may retain a limited right of supervision over it. As it is thus subordinate to the Sovereign, the actual form of the government is a matter of secondary importance, varying according to particular circumstances and needs of men. Rousseau says that men must never forget that they come together for the sake of good life and should do nothing to make that good life impossible. If the state acts immorally it is denying itself and is not a true state[16].

Rousseau believes that only where the General Will reigned could man's nature be developed and man could attain his full stature only in the great community of the state. Rousseau's work is the reassertion of the Aristotelian view that man is a political animal whose nature can be fulfilled only in the state, which is not the result of his vice but the condition of his virtue, the chief agent of morality.

Modern Theories of International Human Rights

The modern theories of Human Rights have been developed either as a reaction to the earlier ones or as the refinements to the existing jurisprudence on human rights. Among them must be mentioned John

Rawls, Nozik, Modougal and Dworkin. These theories display a number of common characteristics:

- First, they are eclectic, benefiting from each other's insights. It is imprecise to characterize these theories as simply utilitarian, natural rights, intuitive or behavioural.
- Secondly, modern theorists recognize and try to address, using various approaches, the tension between liberty and equality. Some do so through theories of resolution, which try to show that these goals are reconcilable and achievable within the same social order. Some find the tension irreconcilable and seek to resolve the dilemma by ranking goals hierarchically. Others evolve refining theories which accept a relationship between liberty and equality characterized by shifting readjustments[17].
- Thirdly, most theorists acknowledge the need to construct an entire system of rights.

The Modern Theories of Human Rights in the second half of the twentieth century has come to mean defense of the rights of human beings against abuses of power committed by the organs of the state with the help of institutionalized means. It also involves the promotion of the establishment of human living conditions and the overall development of the human personality.

The Modern Theories of Human Rights can be broadly placed under the following categories:

- Theories based on Core Rights;
- Theories based on the value of Utility;
- Theories based on Justice;
- Theories based on a revisited State of Nature and the Minimalist state;
- Theories based on Dignity; and
- Theories based on Equality.[18]

The main contentions of these theories are as such:

- First, the validity of human rights is established by *specific legislation.*

- Second, within the bourgeois legal system the human rights issue receive an extended treatment by two branches of law, i.e. *Constitutional and International Law.*
- Third, human rights are vested in all individuals and only in individuals and not in professional groups. Furthermore, a human being enjoys his or her human rights both as an individual and a citizen.
- Fourth, the human rights concept remains immutably valid where ever human beings live a collective life.

Views of Rawls

John Rawls's (b. 1921) *A Theory of Justice* (1971) is regarded as his most significant contribution to political philosophy. Rawls's political thought has been concerned with the problem of providing a justification for political liberalism. In his *Theory of Justice* he attempts to reconcile a liberal ideal of political obligation with a redistributionist conception of social justice. Rawls conception of justice has deep roots in the liberal democratic tradition. Rawls extensively made use of traditional device of the *Social Contract* as a means of establishing his theory of justice. By reviving the idea of social contract, Rawls placed himself within the tradition of Locke, Rousseau and Kant.[19]

Like the traditional theory of social contract, Rawls referred to a hypothetical situation to construct his theory of justice. Rawls emphasized on the 'circumstances of justice' referring to man's natural situation, what he called "initial position" in which they are bounded by incomplete knowledge and limited judgement.[20] He advocated that this initial situation must be characterized in such a way that it would lead to a certain conception of justice. However according to Rawls, the genuine principle of justice are the outcome of rational human decision. In fact, the choice of the principles of justice are the result of moral deliberation in the sense that in moral debates the participants rise above the consideration of their personal interest, biases and prejudices. Rawls considers 'justice' as ' Fairness' as the principles of justice are the outcome of a fair agreement in an initial situation. *Two principles of justice* emerge from Rawls notion of justice which guarantee:

- Equality of political rights as citizens in a democratic country.
- Fair treatment in the distribution of social and economic values.

The first principle implies that each person is to have an equal right to the most extensive basic liberty compatible with similar liberty for others. These basic liberties are essential for the development of individual liberty. Roughly speaking, the basic liberties of citizens are *political liberty* together with *freedom of speech and assembly*, *liberty of conscience* and *freedom of thought, right to hold property* and *freedom from arbitrary arrest.*

The second principle of justice suggests that social and economic inequalities are to be so arranged that they are both:

- To the greatest benefit of the least advantaged; and reasonably expected to be to everyone's advantage.
- Attached to offices and position open to all under the condition of fair equality of opportunity maintaining self-respect of the individual.

Thus under the second principle, inequalities in wealth and income cannot be justified as consequences of the right to property or difference in ability. Income and wealth would have to be distributed equally among citizens unless it could be shown that inequality would benefit everyone.[21] Rawls introduces the conception of 'primary goods' which includes rights, liberties, power, wealth, opportunities and self-respect. A just society is one, he argues, that distributes these primary goods equally among its citizens.[22] Rawls does not allow economic or social gain at the cost of basic liberties. Rawls believes that basic liberties are essential for individuals if a society has to move towards perfection.

Rawls opines that the principles of justice are to be applied to the basic structure of social institutions. He maintains that the principle of justice should give an economic system which regulates the public good. In order to achieve this goal, he argues, it is necessary to organize the social and economic process within suitable political and legal institutions, which he calls 'basic structure of the society'.[23] It is this structure which determines the nature of the state. It is assumed that state is an organization of political power. But political power is not an isolated phenomenon. Its structure is highly blended with economic and social structure.

Rawls projects a model of 'constitutional democracy' as an ideal political system which provides a procedure fulfilling the requirements of equal liberty and an effective system of legislation. Equal liberty is nothing but equal participation. His logic is that as the citizens are expected to obey the laws, they should enjoy equal rights to have better benefit of the constitutional process. The principle of justice, Rawls emphasizes, should also determine an economic system capable of regulating public good. It is necessary to shape the social and economic process within suitable political and legal institutions.

Thus it is evident that Rawls is an egalitarian and an advocator of justified inequality. He asserts that the function of the state is not only to maintain law and order but also to achieve distributive justice by putting the highest social value on the requirements of the disadvantaged. The state regulates the general conditions to facilitate the individuals to pursue their interest and maximizes the conditions for their liberties. Therefore, rights and freedom of individuals, Rawls argues cannot be separated from the state.

POINTS TO REMEMBER

- Human Rights are inherent and inalienable rights, which are due to an individual by virtue of his/her being a human being. These rights have been translated into legal rights, established according to the law-creating processes of societies, both national and international. The basis of these legal rights is the consent of the governed.
- The evolution of the contemporary concept of human rights is commonly understood in terms of three generations of human rights. The first generation rights - were concerned mainly with the civil and political rights of the individual. The second generation rights - provide for social, economic and cultural security. The third generation of human rights - are concerned with rights of groups and peoples rather than of individuals and include such rights as the right to self-determination and the right to development.
- The socio-political theories of Human Rights can be placed under two categories: the Classical Liberal Theories and the Modern International Theories of International Human Rights.
- The Liberal-Individualist Theory of Natural Rights is the earliest theory of rights which gained distinct recognition from the authors of the Social Contract Theory - Hobbes, Locke and Rousseau.

- The modern theories of Human Rights have been developed either as a reaction to the earlier ones or as the refinements to the existing jurisprudence on human rights. They have come to mean defense of the rights of human beings against abuses of power committed by the organs of the state with the help of institutionalized means.

- The modern theories contend that the validity of human rights is established by specific legislation, which receive an extended treatment by two branches of law, i.e. *Constitutional* and *International Law.*

- John Rawls, one of the exponents of the modern theory of human rights attempts to reconcile the liberal ideal of political obligation with a redistributionist conception of social justice. Rawls is an egalitarian and an advocator of justified inequality.

NOTES AND REFERENCES

1. Two important publications which examine the contributions of various streams of thought on Human Rights are: *Human Rights, Comments and Interpretations,* London/New York, Alban Wingate, 1948; and *Birthright of Man,* Paris, UNESCO, 1969.
2. P. Alston (ed.), *The United Nations and Human Rights, A Critical Appraisal,* Oxford, Clarendon Press, 1992, p. 3.
3. Jack Donnelly, "Satisfying Basic Needs in Africa: Human Rights, Markets and State", *Africa Today,* Vol. 32, No. 2, 1985, p. 2.
4. S. Kim, "Global Human Rights and World Order". in: R. Falk, S. Kim and S. Mendlovitz, *The United Nations and a Just World Order,* Colorado, Westview Press, 1991, pp. 368 - 69.
5. J.W. Nicket, *Making Sense of Human Rights,* Berkeley, University of California Press, 1987, pp. 3 - 4.
6. R. Falk, *Human Rights and State Sovereignty,* New York, Holmes and Meier, 1981, p. 6.
7. I. Szabo, "Historical Foundations of Human Rights and Subsequent Developments" in K. Vasak ed., *The International Dimensions of Human Rights,* Paris, UNESCO and Westport, 1982, p. 11.
8. M.S. Mcdougal and Bebr Gerhard, "Human Rights in the United Nations", *American Journal of International Law,* Vol. 56, 1964, p. 604.
9. Maurice Cranston, *Human Rights Today,* Bombay, Manaktalas, 1966, p. 7.
10. Evan Luard, "The Origins of International Concern over Human Rights" in Evan Luard (ed.), *The International Protection of Human Rights,* London, Thames and Hudson, 1967, p. 7.

11. George H. Sabine and Thomas L. Thorson, *A History of Political Thought*, New Delhi, Oxford Publishing Company, 1973, pp. 422 to 440.
12. *Ibid.*, pp. 478 - 499.
13. *Ibid.*
14. *Ibid.*, pp. 529 - 548.
15. *Ibid.*
16. *Ibid.*
17. Gokulesh Sharma, *Human Rights and Legal Remedies*, New Delhi, Deep and Deep Publications, 2000, p. 39.
18. *Ibid.*, p. 40.
19. Peter Lassman, "John Rawls, Justice and a Well Ordered Society", in Leonard Tivey (ed.) *Political Thought Since 1945*. London, 1992, p. 197.
20. *Ibid.*, p. 202.
21. John Rawls, *A Theory of Justice*, Harvard, Harvard University Press, 1971, pp. 11-12.
22. *Ibid.*, p. 62.
23. *Ibid.*

SUGGESTED READINGS

1. A.H. Birch (1993) *The Concepts and Theories of Modern Democracy*, Routledge, London.
2. David Beetham (1995) *Politics and Human Rights*, Basic Blackwell, London.
3. Ernest Barker (1961) *Principles of Social and Political Theory*, Oxford University Press, New Delhi.
4. G. Haragopal (1997) *Political Economy of Human Rights*, Himalaya, Mumbai
5. James Fawcett (1985) *Social Science Encyclopaedia*, Routledge, New Delhi.
6. John Rawls (1971) *A Theory of Justice*, Harvard University Press, Harvard.
7. O.P. Gauba (1995) *An Introduction to Political Theory*, MacMillan, New Delhi.
8. Upendra Baxi (1987) *The Right to be Human*, Lancer International, New Delhi.

MODEL QUESTIONS

Objective Questions (2 Marks Each)

1. In which year did the Bolshevik Revolution take place ?
2. What does WASP stands for ?
3. In which year was Slavery officially abolished in America ?
4. Who were the main exponents of the Social Contract Theory ?

Short Questions (5 Marks Each)

1. Write a brief note on the concept of Human Rights.
2. Briefly discuss the concept of Human Rights in terms of three generations of human rights.

Long Questions (15 Marks Each)

1. Discuss the Liberal - Individualist Theory of Natural Rights with particular emphasis to the views of Hobbes and Locke.
2. Discuss the views of John Rawls in the context of the Modern Theory of Human Rights.

2

APPROACHES AND PERSPECTIVE

Universalistic and Relativist Approaches to Human Rights

Human Rights mean justice, ethical correctness or consonance with the rules of law and the principles of morals. It is considered as the foundation of all rights and moral principles, which impact the character of justice and gives it an ethical context. They are rights which are enjoyed by human beings purely as such, being grounded in personality and existing antecedently to their recognition by positive law. Human Rights are intrinsically bound up with the prevailing social environment and the relationship that exists between man and the institutions at a given time. Like any other social norms, human rights possess historical character. Hence there are different approaches to the understanding of the concept.

Universalistic Approach

The *Magna Carta in England* 1215, the *American Declaration of Independence* 1776, the *Bolshevik Revolution in Russia* 1917, could be cited as important landmarks in the development of the concept of human rights. Each of these declarations has made important contribution in advancing the concept of human rights. However, being product of their own time and specific circumstances they were narrow in their scope and application. Although the Magna Carta set limitations to arbitrary rule and laid the foundation for the rule of law, it yielded certain concessions only for the feudal lords. Similarly the real beneficiaries of the American Declaration and the Bill of Rights were those who constituted what was abbreviated as WASP (White, Anglo-Saxon and Protestant). Slavery continued to be a part of the American social and political system and it was only in 1864 that slavery in America was legally abolished. The French Declaration proclaiming liberty, equality and fraternity for all, to date, represented the most revolutionary social concept yet it did not address the needs of social and economic justice of the working class. By the beginning of the mid-nineteenth century, the demand for economic security and social justice in addition to civil and political rights, appeared in the forefront of socialist movements. Thus the Bolshevik Revolution in Russia (1917) emphasized that economic and social rights were as important as civil and political rights. By the end of the nineteenth century, in Europe and North America, the concept of natural right was secularized, rationalized and democratized. In its place emerged a concept what was called "*the Rights of Man*".

On account of the convergence of several historical factors, by the middle of the twentieth century, a concept of human rights universal in its approach and comprehensive in its content emerged. International concern for human rights found expression in the Charter of the United Nations - the first international instrument which, in unequivocal terms, proclaimed "universal respect for, and observance of, human rights and fundamental freedom for all without distinction as to race, sex, language or religion"[1] . The Charter made promotion of these rights as one of its basic purposes and obligated member states to take joint and separate action in cooperation with the United Nations for the achievement of this purpose. The UN Çharter thus ushered in a new international law of human rights. Until then the question of human rights was considered to be a matter between state and individuals within its territory. As such it was beyond the reach of international law and of no concern to the international community. For the first time in the history of mankind human rights were universalized and internationalized - rights which every individual whatever one's origin could claim as a member of human society.

As the rights laid down in the UN Charter were general in nature, it was therefore deemed necessary to define human rights and fundamental freedoms so that the objectives of the Charter could be pursued and an international system for promotion and protection of human rights could be instituted. After three years of preparatory work, in December 1948, the UN General Assembly proclaimed the Universal Declaration of Human Rights. The Declaration defines specific rights - civil and political as well as economic, social and cultural - with equality and freedom from discrimination as a principal and recurrent theme. It spells out the right to life, liberty and security of person, to fair trial by due process of law, to freedom of conscience, thought, expression, association and privacy, freedom of movement and the right to leave one's country and return to it; right to marriage and family; right to work and leisure, health care and education and so on. What is most significant about the Declaration is that it declares the will of the people to be the basis of the authority of government. The Universal Declaration was not conceived as law but as a "Common standard of achievement" for all peoples of all nations. It stirred the moral consciousness as well as the political assertiveness of people in various countries. Notwithstanding its strong impact and the momentum that it generated worldwide for observation and protection of human rights, the Declaration carries no legal sanction to compel states to meet the obligation of ensuring observance and implementation of human rights enshrined in the Declaration. Beginning 1947, efforts were directed to seek a legal framework and to convert the norms set in the Declaration into legally binding obligations. Eventually, after twenty years of preparatory work accompanied by protracted debates, negotiations and compromises to accommodate differing views, the General Assembly promulgated in December 1966, International Covenants comprising three instruments: *International Covenants on Economic, Social and Cultural Rights; International Covenants on Civil and Political Rights;* and *Optional Protocol* (on individual petition) to the Covenants on Civil and Political Rights. Besides, over the decades, scores of other instruments dealing with specific rights - rights of stateless person, of the refugees, of women, elimination of all forms of discrimination, and so on have also been proclaimed.

It is important to keep in mind the basic point that the notion of human rights is intimately linked to the notion of the "state". It is only in the context of organized society with public authorities, that the notion of human rights makes sense. Human rights thus refer to norms concerning the relationship between individual and the state. What the international system has evolved over the decades, is to obligate states to respect, protect and to implement human rights as internationally agreed upon. The fact that human rights require a set of corresponding duties to the community is also given due acknowledgment. The question of human rights is one of relationship of the individual to his fellow human beings. It is only by proper association with other human beings that an individual can achieve full development of his personality. As such rights imply duties; the later term could also be described as "rights" of the community against the individual. It is being increasingly recognized that rights carry explicit as well as implicit corresponding duties. Rights without emphasis on duties could prove to be counterproductive. Therefore, to emphasize rights unilaterally and to ignore duties would put in jeopardy the network of social relations in a given community. The Universal Declaration reiterates this social reality in Article 2(I) when it states that "everyone has duties to the community in which alone the free and full development of his personality is possible"[2]. On behalf of the community, the state is permitted to impose certain limitations on the human rights system. The same article of the Universal Declaration in paragraph two also lays down that:

> In the exercise of his rights and freedoms everyone shall be subject only to such limitations as are determined by law solely for the purpose of securing due recognition and respect for the rights and freedoms of others and of meeting the just requirements of morality, public order and the general welfare in a democratic society[3].

Similarly, the two Covenants, while enumerating specific rights refer, in their respective preambles, to the duties of the individual to other individuals and to the community to which he belongs. They acknowledge the authority of the state to subject the rights enumerated in the covenants to certain limitations for promoting the general welfare of the society. What is most significant is that the International system of Human Rights envisages that the will of the people shall be the basis of the authority of government. This is the cornerstone of the human rights system, the principle of popular sovereignty, which means that the authority of the state shall be exercised by the will of the people themselves and that their participation in governance shall be truly representative. However, these provisions are not suggestive of any particular form of government, nor do they aim to impose a universal vision of how social order should be organized and secured within a community. They just confine themselves to setting forth an essential principle: in order to ensure the highest probability of an adequate balance between competing interests, as expressed in assertions for rights and freedoms on one hand and demands on the other, it is essential that everyone living within the state should participate on an equal basis in the life of the society. In other words, it implies influencing the exercise of authority and also the formulation of legal norms regulating the scope of freedoms and demands. The international system of human rights, not only include rights and freedoms on the one hand and state obligations on the other, but also includes system of monitoring and supervision at the international level.

Humanitarian intervention at the international level may be considered as an indication of international concern for Human Rights. The real beginning of the development of international protection of Human Rights was made only during the nineteenth century. The League of Nations was established in 1920.The contributions of the International Labour Organization and the Committee on International Intellectual Co-operation and Health Committee under the aegis of the League were equally noteworthy in creating an atmosphere at the international level. However, the outbreak of the Second World War led to the demise of the League. The United Nations was created in 1945 and its Charter accords the highest priority to Human Rights and places it at par with the maintenance of international peace and security. A landmark in the history of international concern for Human Rights was the adoption of Universal Declaration of Human Rights on December 10, 1948. It enjoins the protection of Human Rights by the Rule of Law. In the spirit of the Declaration of Human Rights, the General Assembly of the United Nations adopted the International Covenants of Human Rights.

From the time of the establishment of the United Nations, there has been a tremendous surge in the development of international law. The general human rights concepts embodied in the UN Charter were elaborated in the 1948 Universal Declaration of Human Rights and had a very wide impact influencing the formulation of many new national constitutions and municipal laws. At the international level, the same process has gradually evolved, beginning with the establishment of an International Bill of Rights; to the point where the UN system has developed, standards of human rights in a diverse range of areas and can be regarded as providing a global human rights regime. Additional mechanisms for the protection of human rights also occur at the regional level, through instruments such as *Rights and Fundamental Freedoms, 1950* the *American Convention of Human Rights, 1960*, and the *African Charter on Human and People's Rights, 1981* of the Organization of African Unity. The existence of these instruments and their corresponding enforcement mechanisms reflect the two distinct kinds of activity which have been taking place since the adoption of the Universal Declaration. One is the process of *"political acceptance"* and the other of *"legal codification"*. The "political acceptance" process determines which moral claims based on concepts of human welfare or human need, should be accepted as general standards or statements of principle about human rights. Secondly, there is a process of "legal codification" which translates these principles into legal norms defining specific rights and obligations, capable of implementation through international machinery and procedures. The development of the international law of human rights has been paralleled by a growing public awareness worldwide of the meaning and significance of concepts of human rights which has in turn led to increased recognition by governments both of their internal accountability to the people they govern, and also of the need for "international legitimization" to conform and supplement their political legitimacy at home.

While the internationalization and universalization of human rights may not have made much headway in the actual realization of human rights, its significance lies in the fact that for the first time in the history of mankind there are "rights" which every individual irrespective of his origin, religion, race, colour and nationality can claim as a member of human society. What is more significant is that these human rights are universal and accepted by all states, regardless of their historical, economic, social and cultural differences or ideological persuasions. These rights are civil and political, economic, social and cultural - covering every facet of human life.

Relativist Approach

The concept of Human Rights has been variable and a dynamic one. It has in fact varied from generation to generation and evolved with the changing times and under the constantly shifting conditions. Even within the same society, perception of what human rights are may vary from state to state. Hence, human rights have been classified from various angles. The different facets of classification from different points of view are the following[4]:

- Classification from the historical point of view.
- Classification from the chronological development point of view.
- Classification from the philosophical point of view.
- Classification from social sciences point of view.
- Classification from the enforceability point of view.
- Classification from the point of view of individual and society.
- Classification from geographical point of view.
- Classification from general and specific point of view.

The Universality of human rights does not fit very comfortably in a political order structured around sovereign states. Universal moral rights are better suited to a cosmopolitan conception of world politics, which sees individuals more as members of a single global political community rather than as citizens of states. There are thus three competing theoretical models on the place of human rights in international relations, each with its own conception of the international community and its role in international human rights.

The Traditional Statist Model sees human rights as principally a matter of sovereign national jurisdiction. Contemporary statists acknowledge the fact that human rights are no longer the exclusive preserve of states, and that the state is no longer the sole significant international actor. Nonetheless, statists insist that human rights remain principally a matter of sovereign national jurisdiction and a largely peripheral concern of international relations. For statists, there is no significant, independent international community.

The Cosmopolitan Model starts with individuals rather than states. This model focuses on challenges to the state and its powers both from below, by individuals and non-government organizations, and not merely international organizations and other groupings of states. They often see international organizations, and even some transnational NGO's as representatives of an inchoate global community of humankind above the society of states. International action on behalf of human rights is relatively unproblematic in such a model. In fact, cosmopolitans largely reverse the burden of proof, requiring justification for non-intervention in the face of gross and persistent violation of human rights.

The Internationalist Model lays stress on the evolving consensus among states and nonstate actors alike on international human rights norms. Without denying the continued centrality of states, internationalists focus attention on the international society of states, which imposes only limited restrictions on states. According to this model, the "international community" is essentially the society of states supplemented by NGO's and individuals, to the extent that they have been formally or informally incorporated into the international political processes. International human rights activity is permissible only to the extent authorized by the formal or informal norms of the international society of states.

Each of the above mentioned models can be viewed as resting on descriptive claims about the place that human rights do have in contemporary international relations or prescriptive claims about the place they ought to have. For instance, the statist model may argue descriptively that human rights are in fact peripheral in international relations, or prescriptively that they ought to be peripheral, or both. The cosmopolitan model, however, have little descriptive power. States and their interests in fact still dominate contemporary international relations. Although the international political power of individuals, NGO's, and other nonstate actors is real, it is still relatively small and essentially a relative notion. The global political community is at best rudimentary. The cosmopolitan model, to that extent is largely a prediction about the direction of change in world politics. The internationalist model provides the most accurate description of the place of human rights in contemporary international relations. The current descriptive power of an internationalist model, however, does not imply that it will necessarily remain accurate in the future.

The exponents of the *relativist approach* to Human Rights argue that moral values are historically and culturally specific rather than universal. They point out that there are a variety of distinctive and defensible conceptions of human rights that merit respect and toleration. One standard form of such arguments has been the claim that there are "three worlds" of human rights. The *First World* or the "Western" approach, emphasizes on civil and political rights and the right to private property. The *Second World* or the "socialist" approach emphasizes on economic and social rights. The *Third World* approach emphasizes on self-determination and economic development. Both the socialist and the Third World conceptions are held to be group oriented, in contrast to the fundamental individualism of the "Western" approach. It is evident that political histories, cultural legacies, economic conditions, and issues of human rights differ in the three "Worlds". There is considerable diversity even within each "World" especially the Third World. Cultural relativity is a fact. Social institutions and values have varied and continue to vary, with time and place[5].

Moral relativism emphasizes on moral values and thus conceptions of human rights are determined by history, culture, economics or some other independent social force and is best seen as a matter of degree. At one extreme is *radical relativism* that sees culture as the source of all values. Such a position in effect denies the very idea of human rights, for it holds that there are no rights that everyone is entitled to equally, simply as a human being. At the other end of the spectrum lies what may be called *radical universalism,* the view that all values, including human rights, are entirely universal, in no way subject to modification in light of cultural or historical differences. Whatever the possible theoretical attractions of such a view, it has little practical relevance as to insist that all human rights be implemented in precisely identical ways in all countries would be unrealistic. Rejecting the two end points of the spectrum still leaves room for a variety of relativist positions that can be divided into two categories. *Strong relativism* holds that human rights and other values are principally but not entirely determined by culture or other circumstances. On the other hand *weak relativism* reverses the emphasis. Human rights are held to be largely universal, subject only to secondary cultural modifications.

It has been argued that the possibility of justifiable modifications must not obscure the fundamental universality of international human rights norms. Deviations should be rare and their cumulative impacts relatively minor. This suggests that as human rights are specified in greater detail, there is more latitude for legitimate variation. There are three levels at which human rights can be specified. At the top are the "concepts" where very little cultural variability is justifiable. Below these are "interpretations" which gives scope for interpretative variability. At the third level, considerable variation in the particular form in which an interpretation is implemented may be justifiable.

Feminist Perspective on Human Rights

Both in Vienna at the UN World Conference on Human Rights in 1993 and in Beijing at the UN World Conference on Women in 1995 women's rights were recognized as human rights. For the first time their articulation was accepted as an aspect of international human rights law. The underpinning of women's rights with human rights gave women's rights discourse a special trajectory, emerging as a major innovation of human rights policy within the framework of international law. However, relative to other fields, women's rights are more fragile, have weaker implementation procedures, and suffer from inadequate financial support from the United Nations.

There are historical reasons why the claim that women's rights are human rights has gained ascendancy in the world today. "Rights offer a recognized vocabulary to frame political and social wrongs"[6]. Women are increasingly using this vocabulary to articulate their grievances. The availability of human rights discourse for the translation of women's rights into internationally acceptable norms allows for a greater visibility for the issues of women's rights. In addition, the diverse machinery set up at the international level for the promotion of human rights now remains available for women's rights activists. This access to international machinery of implementation is also an important development in the search for women's equality.

In earlier times the relationship between international human rights law and women's issues was not a happy one. International human rights law has been subjected to a feminist critique. Such law was, it was argued, state centered and individualistic in content. Its structure and appeal was basically towards male subjects, with only passing reference to women's inequality. Most importantly, international human rights law reinforced the division between the public world and private life. By insulating the internal practices of states from scrutiny, it ensured that community and private life continued without any reference to international standards. There was considered to be a public sphere where the state and the international system may intervene and a private sphere where state intervention and international scrutiny were prohibited. It was assumed that privacy was a neutral, powerless realm of human experience, and that there was no power hierarchy within the private space of the family. Critics have argued that the absence of legal intervention to protect women in the community and in the home devalued women's roles and kept the traditional male-dominated hierarchy of the family intact.

The founding theorists of international law were all male and did not recognize the political nature of private life[7]. In international law as in political life generally, much depends on who controls the influential discourses[8]. Men formulated and to date actually control international mechanisms of implementation. This corresponds to the privileging of public life over the personal. In addition the state was the primary, sovereign actor in international law. Intervention in the activities of the nation - state was absolutely unacceptable until a few years ago. This sovereignty ensured that community and private life located within the jurisdiction of the nation state were secluded from scrutiny.

The roots of this state - centeredness in international law and international human rights law lie in the liberal theories of social contract that privilege the negative minimalist state rather than the interventionist one. In addition, the rise of totalitarianism in Europe in the forms of fascism and communism led many to stress the protection of private life by insulating it from activity in the public sphere. By carving out a special area for private expression there were necessary safeguards aimed at preventing the totalitarian state from destroying the dignity of human beings. Liberal theory of the minimalist state and fear of state monopoly of private life contributed to the rigid dichotomy between the public and the private, a dichotomy that until recently was the unshakable foundation of international law in general and international human rights in particular.

A revolution has taken place in the last decade. Women's rights have been catapulted on to the human rights agenda with a speed and determination that has rarely been matched in international law. There are two aspects to this process: first, the attempt to make mainstream human rights responsive to women's concerns; and second, the conceptualization of certain gender-specific violations as human rights violations. These developments have far-reaching implications for the theory and practice of human rights in the United Nations system. The major turning point, was the UN Conference on Human Rights in Vienna in 1993. The Women's lobby at this Conference had an important impact. Their lobbying effort succeeded. Article 18 of the Vienna Declaration and Programme of Action states:

> The human rights of the girl child are an inalienable, integral and indivisible part of universal human rights. The full and equal participation of women in political, civil, economic, social and cultural life, at the national, regional and international levels, and the eradication of all forms of discrimination on grounds of sex are priority objectives of the international community ... The human rights of women should form an integral part of the United Nations activities, including the promotion of all human rights instruments relating to women.

The striking growth of the women's movement is an important factor in international politics today. It points to the significance of international civil society as an initiator of programmes and mechanisms in the UN system[9]. The Women's lobby is made up of an international coalition of women's groups that have focused their energies and efforts in addressing issues of concern to women. Distinct lobbies have made up the whole. There is the *humanitarian women's lobby, which* is particularly interested in the problems of violence against women in armed conflict. *A second lobby of African and Asian* women have been interested in health problems and customary practices that are violent towards women. The *third lobby of North American, European and Latin American Women* has been interested in the issues of domestic violence, rape and sexual harassment. Another lobby that has played a major part in these international initiatives was *Women Living under Muslim Laws,* which has made a strong case for including the violation of women's rights resulting from religious extremism as a major area of concern. Finally, *a lobby* from *Southeast and East Asia* has dealt with the problem of trafficking and forced prostitution. It has been very active at both the regional and national level.

NGO lobbies have truly assisted UN value formation. This activist role for international civil society actors marks a major step forward in the process of creating normative international standards. Women transcending national boundaries in search of international protection are part of parallel developments in other areas of human rights. The dynamic growth of human rights law in the past two decades has challenged the hegemony of the nation-state and the sanctity of sovereign borders. The internal practices of states have become an important concern of the international community.

The discourse on women's rights has transformed the basic tenets of international law. It is often said that civil and political rights are the first generation of human rights; economic, social and cultural rights are the second generation; and group right and the right to self-determination are considered to be the third generation. It may be argued that women's rights are the fourth generation, radically challenging the private - public distinction in international human rights law and pushing for the rights of sexual autonomy. One way in which human rights doctrine is being transformed is through a radical reinterpretation of the earlier generation of rights to meet the concerns of women. For example, the rights to life and freedom from torture are being invoked as new rights that should be reexamined in light of violence against women. Feminist writings examine the question of equality, a cardinal principle of human rights and the first step in the recognition of women's rights. These writings have experimented with the concept to bring in the issue of difference - the special quality of being female as an aspect that should be respected by the principle.[10] In other words they want the human rights concept of equality to include and understand gender difference. It is argued that sex-specific violations should gain visibility as an aspect of equality in the world of international human rights. Masculine and feminine are differences that require analysis and conceptualization without making them hierarchical.[11] Women's experiences are different and women's rights should learn to respect these differences without resorting to male privilege. Women's groups argue that pluralism is necessary but must be built on a firm foundation of human rights. The notion of choice is integral to human rights understanding of the issue of cultural pluralism. Diversity should be celebrated only if those enjoying their cultural attributes are doing so voluntarily. By protecting choice, voluntariness, and the integrity of female decision-making, feminists believe that the dilemma between cultural diversity and the need for the protection of women's human rights may be reconciled.

Human rights discourse is a powerful tool for critiquing states. The discourse has nearly universal acceptance and carries with it an air of universality and legitimacy. However, when it comes to women's rights, in many societies human rights are actually weak discourse in the context of family and community relations. It is this weakness which is a cause of concern for feminists, because regardless of all the international standards and accompanying national legislation unless there is resonance in national civil societies there is little scope for real transformation.

Marxist Perspective on Human Rights

The Marxist perspective on human rights can be traced to the writings of Karl Marx, F. Engles, V.I. Lenin and a host of other thinkers broadly belonging to the Marxist School of Thought. Marxist theory repudiates the liberal notion of atomized and alienated individual, motivated by enlightened self-interest. It insists on the social nature of man who lives in a co-operative network of human relationships. Rights, for Marx, are the products of Capitalist society, which are designed to maintain the privileges of the ruling classes.[12] In the Communist society where everyone realizes one's creative potential, rights are no longer needed.

The Marxian concept of human rights puts emphasis on social rights rather than individual rights. Dominated by the writings of Marx, the argument runs that full realization of an individual's self is possible only within the context of a society. In as much as an individual should be concerned with his development, the society has an interest in facilitating the advancement of individuals. The overwhelming responsibility of the state towards its subjects demands that economic and social rights should have predominance over the individual ones. Such a conceptualization of the nature of society precludes the existence of individual rights rooted in the state of nature, which are prior to the state.

Marx is critical of liberal views of human rights. Making a scathing attack on the concept of natural rights, Marx in his 'On the Jewish Question', considers it as the ideological expression of bourgeois egoism and social atomization.[13] The so called rights of man, Marx points out, are nothing but the rights of egoistic man, of man separated from other men and, from the community. Marx goes on to extend his basic postulate by emphasizing the necessary connection between bourgeois society and the notion of human rights.

Writing in the *Holy Family,* Marx and Engels, further state that the recognition of the rights of man by the modern state has no other meaning than the recognition of slavery by the ancient state. The individual man in the modern state is linked with other men only by the ties of private interest and unconscious natural necessity. It follows that the very notion of human rights, according to Marx and Engels is linked to the competitive struggle that is the hallmark of the bourgeois society and is based on the vision of society and the individual as inherently separate and antagonistic units. Human rights are thus viewed as instruments for carrying out adversary relations between competing, primarily atomistic individuals. Marx points out that the process of bourgeois exploitation holds the entire society at the mercy of market forces. It has an alienating, depersonalizing and dehumanizing impact on man. The institutionalized imposition of the capitalist will on man alienates him from his nature besides alienating him from his activity, himself and from other men.

For Marx society does not consist of relations between individual and individual but between classes be it the farmer and landlord or worker and capitalist. Marx believed that the alienation of man could end only with the establishment of Communism - when classes have been eliminated, exploitation has ceased and the state has withered away. Class struggle would eventually result in the victory of the working class and it was only then that exploitation would come to an end. Marx depicted Communism as the fulfillment of the individualistic goals which liberalism had proclaimed but had been unable to realize. Thus it was the nature of the community that determined the rights and fate of man. It was only in a communistic community that man could be a true individual. With the workers obtaining effective control over the means, conditions and results of their labour, the process of controlling the immediate direct political power in the society would reach its logical culmination.

Two points need to be noted. First, the Marxist perspective on rights has been successful in highlighting the socio-economic freedoms and the concept of equality, which was largely ignored by the liberal theory. Second, the neo-Marxists have begun to recognize the emancipatory potential of rights to better the livelihoods of the marginalized. Rights, in Marxist-Leninist doctrine comes from law, which comes from government and which reflects the underlying economic relationships of any society. As rights are derived from a fundamental economic relationship, from the place of the individual in a pattern of production, it is not surprising that economic and social rights are taken to come before civil and political rights.

Third World Perspective on Human Rights

The diverse socio-cultural matrix of developing countries does not permit them to approach the promotion and protection of human rights, in a thorough and unified way. Nor can they be guided by the Western style ideology and thinking on protection of human rights. This is on account of three reasons. *First,* the incorporation of Western theories of human rights would amount to the continuation of the colonial heritage. *Secondly,* as most of the countries of the Third World are in a flux, any kind of incorporation of the human rights regime determined by the West would be either inappropriate or too rigid for these countries. *Thirdly,* the politicization of human rights has made the ruling elite's of the Third World highly suspicious of the Western notion of human rights.

As a matter of fact, developing countries show a remarkable difference of cultures and socio-economic realities *inter-se* and *intra-se.* They also represent the world's major religions and political ideologies. At the same time they are faced with tremendous problems of state building, economic reconstruction and regional, sub-regional and ethnic conflicts. These conflicts have the potential to threaten the very foundation of the state. Even within the Third World, there remains a sharp disagreement on the exact scope and nature of basic human rights, on the treatment of substantive human rights, economic issues and the methodology of protection of these human rights. More often than not the nature of conflict between liberty, equality and other competing values is easily discernible and is prone to many distortions. Three reasons can be attributed to it. *Firstly,* the primary aim of most Third World countries is to strengthen the authority of the state. It is feared that full recognition of rights and freedoms of individuals would encourage centrifugal tendencies. *Secondly,* in the post-decolonization era the demands of reconstruction and economic development call for a strong government. *Thirdly,* the complex social structure of these countries lays the ground for the government or leader to exercise undisputed powers. Thus the freedom - authority dialectic operative in the Western tradition is alien to the cultures operating in the developing countries.[14]

Over the years, three distinct legal systems have evolved in the Third World. The *first* may be described as an absolutely autocratic state, which does not show any regard towards the promotion and protection of human rights. Being based on the tradition of ruler-ruled relationship, the ruler is deemed to be above law. This is particularly true of some Asian and African countries. *The second category* comprises of countries with progressive regimes, which aim at rapid economic and social transformation and have *de jure* or *de facto* one party rule. But over the years, these countries have faced grave challenges to the one party authority from groups and sub-groups, representing various shades of opinion and ideologies thus forcing governments to adopt tough measures, which has resulted in human rights violation. *The third group* of countries constitute the countries having democratic rules and institutions with two or multi-party system besides having written constitutions and an independent judiciary. These countries are committed to the promotion and protection of human rights enshrined in their constitutions. However the working of these countries have not shown any praise worthy results. The reality of the socio-economic backwardness of a large population puts a premium on the protection of human rights. As most of these societies are faced with the demands of large groups and sub-groups, a homogeneous approach to the protection of human rights becomes difficult.[15]

Throughout the world at all stages of history there seems to have been difficulties in evolving a particular theory and model for human rights protection. This is true for the developed West as well as the developing countries. Not withstanding the core concern shown by international declarations and principles upon protection of human rights, it is difficult to arrive at a concept of human rights in developing countries, which is unanimously acceptable. Nor is there a common framework of action. Faced with immense under-development, combined with foreign and colonial exploitation, poverty and illiteracy, human rights are illusory to large sections of population of these countries. In the process of pursuing socio-economic goals, the developing countries do not show the desired respect to civil and political rights. It is being increasingly recognized that the present international economic system is largely responsible for underdeveloped conditions in the Third World. In this connection it is instructive to refer to the efforts undertaken by developing countries and United Nations Conference on Trade and Development (UNCTAD) to modify the conditions of international economic relations to the advantage of the developing world. New forms of economic dependency have been thrust upon the developing nations by the International Monetary Fund (IMF) and World Bank sponsored structural adjustment programmes. These programmes have forced the developing nations to change their economic policies resulting in the marginalization of large sections of their populations.

Human rights violation is a common feature in most of the developing world where criminalization of politics and lack of accountability has become the order of the day. The brutalization of state power is reflected in the form of state repression with little comfort from the judiciary. Apart from occasional outbursts from the judiciary, press, human rights activists and non-governmental organizations, there is no meaningful attempt to formulate a clear-cut methodology for the protection of human rights. However, for a balanced approach it is imperative that the issues of human rights in the Third World particularly the Afro-Asian and Latin American countries are viewed in the broader context. Any attempt to delink its various dimensions, including the external factors responsible for large-scale repression, denial of rights of national self-determination would be a grave blunder. There is an extremely close nexus between human rights and peace, freedom, national self-determination, economic, cultural and technological development. It is noteworthy that the United Nations and its various agencies have acknowledged the inalienable link between human rights and the major concerns of modern times - freedom, peace, development and disarmament.. The adoption of three important international covenants on Economic, Social, Cultural and Political rights in 1976 filled the large void in the movement for human rights. Also, the provisions contained in Articles 22 and 28 are of special significance for the realization of human rights in the Third World.

Views of Gandhi

M.K. Gandhi's view on human rights was a part and parcel of his overall philosophy of life. The coherent vision of Gandhian thought is reflected in two aspects, in his critique of the modern civilization, and in his search for alternatives to the present structures such as the state, technology and property. These two aspects of his thought are complementary and inseparable. Gandhi challenged the foundations of modern civilization. The sophisticated, technological, aggressive and lustful aspects of modern Western civilization repelled him. According to him the industrial civilization of the Occident was based on the exploitation of weaker peoples. Its implicated material life was inconsistent with high thinking. The modern civilization therefore was equivalent to darkness and disease. Gandhi, hence, provided a return to nature like Plato, Rousseau and Tolstoy and said that true civilization consists not in the accumulation of commodities but in a deliberate and voluntary reduction of wants. Gandhi prophesied the decline and doom of Western civilization but he had tremendous faith in the rejuvenating power of the human spirit and firmly held that non-violence could provide a healing tonic to modern civilization. Gandhi accepted the spiritual orientation of politics, sociology and economics.

The central evils against which Gandhi fought were racialism, imperialism, communalism and untouchability. In South Africa he fought against the racially discriminatory policies of the Whites. In India, as a reformer, he fought against the social injustices, tyrannies and oppressions. Gandhi believed that the first condition of non-violence was justice in every department of life. According to him no one could be actively non-violent and not rise against social injustices. He condemned British imperialism as it had resulted in the political and economic subjugation of India. Gandhi further argued that the subordination of life to materialism had led Western democracies to the exploitation of the colonial world. He was against the imperialistic exploitation of the peoples of Asia and Africa by the democracies of the West and identified the rise of Nazism and Fascism as a culmination of this process in Western democracy.[16]

Gandhi believed in truth and non-violence and accepted the creative force of religion in human history. Religion signified to him, belief in the ordered moral governance of the world. Although he called himself a Hindu, he was no narrow sectarian. He was above the bonds of creed, cult, rituals and ceremonies. He accepted the spiritual and moral essence of Hinduism, which according to him was the essence of all the great religions of mankind. True religion, according to him implied an emphasis on the moral values of man as spirit. As soon as the moral values were lost one ceased to be religious. The true religious attitude, to Gandhi, meant the voluntary acceptance and enthusiastic fulfillment of the duties that naturally came one's way. Religion according to him was not merely a means for personal purification but it was an immensely powerful social bond. Gandhi believed that the psychological cleansing of the moral structure of society would result in the elimination of those gross superstitions and customs, which have usurped the place of true religion. Religion according to him was the sense of philanthropy, forbearance, justice, fraternity, peace and all-embracing love, which alone was the basis of the existence of the world.

Gandhi was a moral individualist. He emphasized the dignity and sanctity of the conscience of the individual. He would not sanction any coercion for making people good. The individual seeking to better his character by moral techniques is the starting-point of Gandhian ethics. Gandhi's antipathy to all forms of power is reflected in his ideas on the state and property. The state to him represented "violence in a concentrated form"[17]. He preferred man to live by the exercise of his will than by force of habit. He believed in *Swaraj* a condition in which the individual would be the complete master of himself. Gandhi believed that "no society can possibly be built on a denial of individual freedom. It is contrary to the very nature of man".[18]

Gandhi launched a vigorous attack on the concentration of power in the state. He did not mind so long as the state confined itself to the maintenance of law and order and allowed full scope for voluntary activities of the members. He was convinced that individual freedom alone could make a man voluntarily surrender himself completely to the service of the society. Gandhi argued that freedom lay at the root of progress. An ideal social order, according to him was one in which there was no distinction of high or low and "in which each is guaranteed the fruits of his labour on the one hand and prevented from pressing upon his neighbour on the other".[19] Gandhi's argument against centralization was a moral argument, based on the idea that centralization of power destroyed man's urge to see his own *Swaraj,* in terms of his distinct genius. Decentralization, Gandhi believed, would induce people to realize their responsibility and be non-violent. It was based on a notion of cooperation and social feeling. Gandhi pleaded for decentralization of power in society by the introduction of the system of *panchayat raj* turning each village or units of villages into a republic. This he thought was the only means for ensuring variety and freedom on the one hand, and preventing bureaucratic oppression on the other.

Gandhi inculcated the revolutionary doctrine of equality of wages for the lawyer, the doctor, the teacher and the scavenger. He pointed out that the individualistic propensity towards the acquisition of wealth was the root cause of all evil in the society. Hence he advocated that rich men should recognize the immanence of god in all creatures and should take the initiative in dispossession with a view to the diffusion of universal contentment. This would effect genuine transformation of the society. A really egalitarian society based on mutual active love and harmony was his goal. Gandhi took an evolutionary approach to history. Neither an individual nor a society could take a revolutionary leap and overturn the fundamental pattern of its action.

Gandhi wanted spiritualization of politics. He condemned bitterly western democratic politics because they were infected with threefold contradictions. They believed in limitless expansion of capitalism and this resulted in exploitation of weaker people. Politically, democracy implied scrupulous exactness in dealing with opponents. Economically it meant that the weakest should have the same opportunity as the strongest. Democracy and violence could not be reconciled. He wanted India to evolve 'True Democracy'. However, he wanted progressive approximation to true democracy without violence. Decentralization of power was a key-concept in his theory of democracy.

The Gandhian philosophy of *Satyagraha* is a natural outcome from the supreme concept of truth. *Satyagraha* means the exercise of the purest soul force against all injustice, oppression and exploitation. Satyagraha is an inherent birth right of a person. Gandhi was a believer in the superiority of the soul. He would never sanction any submission to any law if it conflicted with the moral stature of man. The dictates and commands of any government, if they conflicted with the sense of higher duty of a person, had to be resisted. *Satyagraha* was a spiritualized and moralized form of the concept of resistance. To Gandhi freedom was a whole. It was a process of growth in quest of an articulated system of coherent moral purposes and action. A man who obtains freedom over his passions would not tolerate the social and economic exploitation of others, as he would regard them as an extension of the self.

POINTS OF REMEMBER

- Human Rights are intrinsically bound up with the prevailing social environment and the relationship that exists between man and the institutions at a given time. Like any other social norms, human rights possess historical character. Hence there are different approaches to the understanding of the concept.
- Human Rights are Universal and accepted by all states, regardless of their historical, economic, social and cultural differences or ideological persuasions. The international system of human rights, not only include rights and freedoms on the one hand and state obligations on the other, but also includes system of monitoring and supervision at the international level.
- The Relativist approach to human rights argues that moral values are historically and culturally specific rather than Universal. According to them there are a variety of distinctive and defensible conceptions of human rights that merit respect and toleration. Human Rights thus are a variable and dynamic concept.
- The growth of the Women's movement is an important factor in international politics today. It has resulted in the reinterpretation of human rights from the gender perspective by making mainstream human rights responsive to women's concerns.
- The Marxian concept of human rights puts emphasis on social rights rather than individual rights. Rights, in Marxist- Leninist doctrine comes from law, which comes from government and which reflects the underlying economic relationships in any society. Marx depicted Communism as the fulfillment of the individualistic goals which liberalism had proclaimed but had been unable to realize.
- The diverse socio-cultural matrix of the Third World countries does not permit them to approach the promotion and protection of human rights, in a unified manner. Nor can they be guided by the Western style ideology and thinking on the protection of human rights on account of the differences in culture and socio-economic realities. It is being increasingly acknowledged that there is an extremely close nexus between human rights and peace, freedom, national self-determination, economic, cultural and technological development.
- Gandhi's view of human rights was a part and parcel of his overall philosophy of life. The coherent vision of Gandhian thought is

reflected in two aspects, in his critique of the modern civilization, and in his search for alternatives to the present structures such as the state, technology and property. Gandhi was a moral individualist. He believed in the dignity and sanctity of the conscience of the individual.

NOTES AND REFERENCES

1. For comprehensive analysis of UDHR, see *Basic Facts About the United Nations*, Department of Public Information, United Nations, New York, 1994.
2. *Ibid.*
3. *Ibid.*
4. The subject 'Human Rights' has been treated in a detailed manner in *The Encyclopedia Britannica*, Vol. 20, (1985) pp. 713 - 721. The chapter deals in a comprehensive manner the historical development of the concept, the philosophical background, the evolution of three generational rights, 'human rights and the UN', as well as the regional perspectives of human rights.
5. *Ibid.*
6. R.J. Cook(ed.), *Human Rights of Women : National and International Perspectives*, Philadelphia, University of Pennsylvania Press, 1994, p. 61.
7. *Ibid.*, p. 94.
8. *Ibid.*
9. *Ibid.*, p. 159.
10. Martha Minow, *Making All the Difference: Inclusion and Exclusion and American Law*, Ithaca, NY: Cornell University Press, 1990.
11. Marge Schuler (ed.), *From Basic Needs to Basic Rights*, Washington, D.C.: Women's Law and Development Institute, 1995, p. 369.
12. For details see, K. Marx and F. Engles, *On the Jewish Questions*, Collected Works, Moscow, Progress Publishers, 1975.
13. *Ibid.*
14. Samuel P. Huntington, *Political Order in Changing Societies*, New Haven, Yale University Press, 1968.
15. For details see Bjorn Hettne, *Development Theory and the Three Worlds*, Essex : Longman Scientific and Technical, 1990, pp. 190-2.
16. *Harijan*, 18 May 1940.
17. *Harijan*, 1 Feb. 1942.
18. *Works*, Vol. 73, pp. 93-94.
19. *Works*, Vol. 73, pp. 93-94.

SUGGESTED READINGS

1. Amartya Sen (2000), *Development as Freedom*, Oxford India Paperbacks, New Delhi.

2. Atul Kohli (1991), *Democracy and Discontent*, Princeton University Press, New York.
3. J. Waldron(ed.) (1984), *Theories of Rights*, OUP, London.
4. Manoranjan Mohanty (1990), *People's Right*, Sage, New Delhi.
5. Manoranjan Mohanty (2000), *Contemporary Indian Political Theory*, Sanskriti, New Delhi.
6. N. Stammers (1993), *Human Rights and Power*, Political Studies, London.
7. P. Alston(ed.), 1992, *The United Nations and Human Rights, A Critical Appraisal*, Clarendon Press, Oxford.
8. Ratna Kapoor and Brenda Corssman (1996), *Subversive Sites: Feminist Engagements with Law in India*, Sage, New Delhi.
9. Samuel P. Huntington (1991), *Political Order in Changing Societies*, Yale University Press, New Haven.
10. V.R. Mehta (1999), *Foundations of Indian Political Thought*, Manohar, New Delhi.

MODEL QUESTIONS

Objective Questions (2 Marks Each)

1. In which year and in which country was the Magna Carta adopted ?
2. What kind of rights were emphasized by the Bolshevik Revolution ?
3. What is the significance of December 10, 1948 ?
4. What do you mean by Cultural Relativism?

Short Questions (5 Marks Each)

1. Briefly discuss the Universalistic Approach to Human Rights.
2. Highlight the main features of the Marxist Perspective on Human Rights.

Long Question (15 Marks Each)

1. Critically discuss the Feminist Perspective on Human Rights.
2. Briefly outline Gandhi's views on Human Rights.

3

UNITED NATIONS AND HUMAN RIGHTS

UN Charter and the Universal Declaration of Human Rights

The first international treaties concerning human rights were linked with the acceptance of freedom of religion (e.g. the Treaties of Westphalia of 1648) and the abolition of slavery. Slavery had already been condemned by the Congress of Vienna in 1815 and a number of international treaties on the abolition of slavery appeared in the second half of the nineteenth century (e.g. the Treaty of Washington of 1862, documents of the Conferences in Brussels in 1867 and 1890 and in Berlin in 1885). Another field of international co-operation was the elaboration of the laws of war (e.g. the Declaration of Paris of 1856, the First Geneva Convention of 1864 and the Second of 1906 and the Hague Conventions of 1899 and 1907). The creation of the International Committee of the Red Cross in 1864 contributed greatly to these developments.

Since the end of the First World War, there has been a growing belief that governments alone cannot safeguard human rights, which require international guarantees. Though the mandate of the League of Nations, the first universal intergovernmental organization, created after the First World War, did not mention human rights, the League tried to undertake the protection of human rights through international means. However, its concerns were limited mainly to the establishment of certain conditions for the protection of minorities in a few countries.

The standards determining the conditions of industrial workers established in the beginning of the twentieth century became the subject of further international agreements elaborated by the International Labour Organization (ILO), created in 1919. The International Slavery Convention, signed in Geneva on 25 September 1926, ended lengthy efforts aimed at the abolition of slavery. Relevant conventions for the protection of refugees were adopted in 1933 and 1938. However, despite all these developments, human rights law did not emerge in the inter - war period.

The totalitarian regimes established in the 1920s and 1930s grossly violated human rights in their own territories. The Second World War brought about massive abuse of human life and dignity, and attempts to eliminate entire groups of people because of their race, religion or nationality. Thus it became clear that international instruments were needed to codify and protect human rights. This conviction was reflected in and reinforced by the Charter of the United Nations signed on 26 June 1945. The Charter states that the fundamental objective of the Universal organization, namely: 'to save succeeding generations from the scourge of war' and 'to reaffirm faith in fundamental human rights, in the dignity and worth of the human person and in the equal rights of men and women'[1]. Article 1 of the Charter states that one of the aims of the United Nations is to achieve international co-operation in 'promoting and encouraging respect for human rights and for fundamental freedoms for all without distinction as to race, sex, language or religion', thus enshrining the principle of non-discrimination. Article 55 expresses a similar aim, and by Article 56 all members for the United Nations 'pledge themselves to take joint and separate action in co-operation with the Organization for the achievement of the purposes set forth in Article 55'[2].

The provisions of the Charter have the force of positive international law because the Charter is a treaty and therefore a legally binding document. All United Nations member States must fulfil in good faith the obligations they have assumed under the Charter of the United Nations, including the obligations to promote respect for human rights, to promote observance of human rights, and to co-operate with the United Nations and other nations to attain this aim. However, the Charter does not specify human rights and does not establish any specific mechanism to ensure their implementation in Member States.

The task of drawing up an International Bill of Human Rights, defining the human rights and freedoms referred to in the Charter, was charged upon the Commission on Human Rights, established in 1945, which is a subsidiary body of the Economic and Social Council (ECOSOC), one of the United Nations principal organs. The Commission on Human Rights was directed to submit proposals, recommendations and reports concerning an international bill of human rights; international conventions on civil liberties, the status of women, freedom of information and similar matters; the protection of minorities etc. The Commission divided its work in three stages: (1) Declaration defining the Fundamental Rights and Freedom (2) An International Convention or Treaty setting forth in precise terms the provisions which governments were willing to accept as legally binding; and (3) To ensure observance of human rights and to deal with violations. After two and a half years of painstaking efforts the Commission under the Chairmanship of Eleanor Roosevelt drafted a Universal Declaration of Human Rights. The Declaration was approved by the General Assembly of the United Nations on December 10, 1948 'as a common standard of achievement for all peoples and nations'.

The Universal Declaration of Human Rights (UDHR) provided the basis for the formulation by the United Nations of covenant and conventions, declarations and recommendations on specific aspects. The rights proclaimed in the Universal Declaration can be broadly divided into two kinds. The *first* refer to civil and political rights, which include: the right to life, liberty, and security of person; freedom from slavery and torture; equality before the law; protection against arbitrary arrest, detention or exile; the right to a fair trial; the right to own property; political participation; the right to marriage; the fundamental freedoms of thought conscience and religion, opinion and expression; freedom of peaceful assembly and association: and the right to take part in the government of his/her country, directly or through freely chosen representatives. The *second* are economic, social and cultural rights, which relate to, amongst others: the right to work; equal pay for equal work; the right to form and join trade unions; the right to an adequate standard of living; the right to education; and the right to participate freely in cultural life[3].

The two broad sets of Human Rights affirmed in the *Universal Declaration* - civil and political rights, and economic, social and cultural rights were elaborated and divided into two covenants - the *International Covenant on Economic, Social and Cultural Rights*, and the *International Covenant on Civil and Political Rights*. These three documents - the *Universal Declaration of Human Rights, the International Covenant on Civil and Political Rights*, and the *International Covenant on Economic, Social and Cultural Rights* - along with two protocols - the *Optional Protocol to the International*

Covenant on Civil and Political Rights, Aiming at the Abolition of the Death Penalty - constitute the International Bill of Human Rights.

The Universal Declaration of Human Rights was the first part of the objective; the other parts, designed to elaborate the content of the provisions of the Declaration, took many years to complete. It was on 16 December 1966, the United Nations General Assembly adopted the two Covenants - the International Covenant on Economic, Social and Cultural Rights (ICESCR) and the International Covenant on Civil and Political Rights (ICCPR) and an Optional Protocol to the ICCPR, allowing for complaints to be mad by individuals on violations of their rights embodied in the Covenants. In adopting these instruments, the international community not only agreed on the content of each right set forth within the Universal Declaration, but also on measures for their implementation. Again, it was in December 1989 that the Second Optional protocol to the ICCPR, aimed at abolishing the death penalty, was adopted by the General Assembly.

The adoption of these two Covenants endorsed the General Assembly resolution of 1950 that 'the enjoyment of civil and political rights and economic, social and cultural rights are interconnected and interdependent.'

The UDHR sets out 30 articles. *Articles 1 and 2* of the Declaration state that "all human beings are born equal in dignity and rights' and are entitled to all the rights and freedoms set forth in the Declaration" without distinction of any kind such as race, colour, sex, language, religion, political or other opinion, national or social origin, property, birth or other status[4].

Articles 3 to 21 of the Declaration set forth the civil and political rights to which all human beings are entitled; including:

- The right to life, liberty and security of person;
- Freedom from slavery and servitude;
- Freedom from torture or cruel, inhuman or degrading treatment or punishment;
- The right to recognition everywhere as a person before the law; the right to an effective judicial remedy; freedom from arbitrary arrest, detention or exile; the right to a fair trial and public hearing by an independent and impartial tribunal; the right to be presumed innocent until proved guilty;

- Freedom from arbitrary interference with privacy, family, home or correspondence; freedom from attacks upon honour and reputation; the right to protection of the law against such attacks;
- Freedom of movement, the right of asylum; the right to a nationality;
- The right to marry and to have a family; the right to own property;
- Freedom of opinion and expression;
- The right to peaceful assembly and association; and
- The right to take part in government and to equal access to public service;

Articles 22 - 27 of the Declaration set forth the economic, social and cultural rights:

- The right to social security;
- The right to work; the right to equal pay for equal work; the right to form and join trade unions;
- The right to rest and leisure;
- The right to a standard of living adequate for health and well-being;
- The right to education; and
- The right to participate in the cultural life of the community;

The concluding *articles, numbers 28 to 30,* recognizing that everyone is entitled to a social and international order in which the human rights set forth in the Declaration may be fully realized; that these rights may only be limited for the sole purpose of securing recognition and respect of the rights and freedoms of others and that each person has duties to the community in which she or he lives[5].

Significance of the Declaration

Although the Universal Declaration of Human Rights is not legally binding, over the years its main principles have acquired the status of standards, which should be respected by all States. When the Declaration was adopted, there were only fifty-eight Member States of the United Nations. Since that time, this number has more than tripled[6]. The continuing impact of the Declaration and the use made of it bears out its universal acceptance, and it has become a common reference in human rights for all nations. The significance of the Declaration can be summed as follows:

- The Declaration of Human Rights was the first of its kind in the history of international organization. The Declaration was a sort of statement of rights considered essential for human development all over the world. Although the Declaration was not binding on the member states; it provided a yardstick by which the progress of the states and people in the field of human rights could be assessed.
- The Declaration became one of the most remarkable developments in the law of nations. Although not to be considered binding as a treaty, it has developed such authority that it not only is a source of law but has come to have the force of law.
- The Declaration has acquired a political and moral authority which is unequalled by any other international instrument with the exception of the Charter itself. No international instrument has ever received the same acceptance on all levels of society.
- Even at the level of international relations, the Declaration has served a very useful purpose. It has often been cited in support of human rights. For example, the Apartheid policy of South Africa was attacked on the ground that it blatantly violated the letter and spirit of the Declaration. Similarly in the Cold War era countries like Bulgaria, Hungary and Rumania were criticized for failing to live up to the commitments of peace treaties as well as the Declaration of Human Rights. Thus, it is evident that the UN has used the Declaration to reinforce its action against certain states on the ground that the violation of human rights impairs the friendly relations among states.
- The Declaration has exercised profound influence on the constitutions of new nations and regional argreements. Thus the constitutions of Indonesia, Syria, El. Salvador, Haiti, Libya, Jordan and numerous other countries have borrowed much from the Declaration. Even in the treaties and regional agreements the influence of the Declaration is quite visible.

In short, though the Declaration has not been invested with legal force, it has proved to be a useful instrument in providing a ready-made statement of human rights acceptable to the majority of the states.

International Conventions and Covenants and Optional Protocol

As already stated, following the adoption of the Universal Declaration of Human Rights, work began on the drafting of the two International Covenants on Human Rights - one on economic, social and cultural rights and the other on civil and political rights - to put into binding legal form the rights proclaimed in the Declaration. The *International Covenant on Economic, Social and Cultural Rights* (ICESCR), the *International Covenant on Civil and Political Rights* (ICCPR) and the *Optional Protocol* to the latter Covenant were adopted unanimously by the General Assembly on 16 December 1966. These instruments, along with the Declaration itself and a second Optional Protocol adopted in 1989, make up what is now widely known as the *International Bill of Human Rights.* The Covenants, unlike the Universal Declaration, are legally binding treaties for those States which are parties to them and they are thus obliged to respect the procedures for their implementation, including the submission of periodic reports on their compliance with their obligations under the covenants.

The Human Rights which the *International Covenant* on Economic, Social and Cultural Rights (ICESCR) seeks to promote and protect are of three kinds. Briefly summarized, they are:

- The right to work in just and favourable conditions;
- The right to social protection, to an adequate standard of living and to the highest attainable standards of physical and mental well-being; and
- The right to education and the enjoyment of benefits of cultural freedom and scientific progress.

The Covenant provides for the progressive full realization of these rights without discrimination of any kind[7]. None of the rights protected under the covenant can be suspended.

The implementation of the ICESCR is overseen by the Committee on Economic, Social and Cultural Rights, which was established by the Economic and Social Council (ECOSOC) in 1985. It is composed of eighteen independent experts nominated and elected by States Parties to the Covenant, who serve in their personal capacities. The Committee publicly examines periodic reports submitted by States Parties, which reflect the measures adopted, and the progress made in meeting their obligations under the Covenant. Representatives from State Parties are entitled to be present when the Committee examines the report and are engaged in constructive dialogue. The Committee also takes account of relevant information from United Nations Specialized Agencies relating to their particular area of expertise, and invites submissions of written and oral statements by non-governmental organizations.

The Committee reports annually to ECOSOC regarding its consideration of the State reports and presents its concluding observations. The latter reflect the main points of discussion, identify positive aspects as well as principal subjects of concern, factors and difficulties impeding the implementation of the Covenant, and put forward suggestions and recommendations. These observations are an important source of public information.

The International Covenant on Civil and Political Rights (ICCPR) elaborates the political and civil rights identified in the Universal Declaration. These include:

- rights to life, privacy, fair trial;
- freedom of religion;
- freedom from torture; and
- equality before law.

Some of the rights can be suspended in times of public emergency which threatens the life of the nation; provided that the derogation will not involve discrimination on grounds of race, colour, sex, language, religion or social origin. Various means are provided for implementation of these rights under the ICCPR. Article 28 of the Covenant provides for the establishment of a *Human Rights Committee* consisting of eighteen independent experts, nominated and elected by States Parties to the Covenant, who serve in their personal capacities. The Human Rights Committee monitors the implementation of the Covenant in the following ways:

- The Committee examines periodic reports from States Parties to the Covenant on their compliance (Article 40) and accordingly gives suggestions and recommendations to the Government concerned on ways in which the Covenant could be better implemented.

- The Committee can consider complaints of one State against another, provided that both have made a special declaration recognizing this role of the Committee under Article 41.
- The Human Rights Committee also interprets the content and meaning of specific articles of the Covenant. These establish the jurisprudence of the Covenant and thus guide the States Parties in their adherence to their obligations under the Covenant.
- The Committee reports annually on its work to the United Nations General Assembly through the Economic and Social council (ECOSOC).

Since the protection of human rights depends ultimately upon compliance at the national level, the power of the Human Rights Committee is limited, as it has no recourse beyond its comments. However, there is a persuasive value derived from the examination of reports in public, as governments are generally sensitive to public exposure to their human rights performance. Moreover, the principal objective of the Committee is to develop a constructive dialogue with Reporting States and thereby promote the compliance of States with the provisions of the Covenant.

Besides the International Bill of Human Rights, there are a large number of conventions, declarations and recommendations adopted by the General Assembly and other legislative bodies of the United nations system which elaborate in more detail the rights set out in the Universal Declaration and the International Covenants, and which also affirm certain rights not specified in the International Bill of Human Rights. The following are some of the important international instruments pertaining to Human Rights:

- *The Convention on the Prevention and Punishment of the Crime of Genocide* was adopted by the United Nations General Assembly in December 1948 and it came into force in 1951. Genocide is defined in the Convention as certain acts 'committed with the intent to destroy, in whole or in part, a national, ethnic, racial or religious group'. Genocide is designated a crime under international law, whether committed in time of war or of peace, and is defined as a crime against humanity.
- *The International Convention on the Elimination of all Forms of Racial Discrimination* came into force in 1969. It represents

the most comprehensive United Nations statement regarding discrimination on the grounds of 'race, colour, descent or national or ethnic origin'.

- *The Convention on the Elimination of All Forms of Discrimination against Women* was adopted by the United Nations General Assembly on 18 December 1979, and entered into force on 2 September 1981. The object of the Convention is to implement equality between men and women and to prevent discrimination against women, in particular such specific forms of discrimination as forced marriages, domestic violence and less access to education, health care and public life as well as discrimination at work. *The Declaration on the Elimination of Violence Against Women,* adopted by the United Nations General Assembly in 1993[8], calls on all states to take measures to prevent and punish violence against women. In March 1994, the Commission on Human Rights established a Special Rapporteur on violence against women, with the mandate to examine the causes and consequences of violence against women.

- *The Convention Against Torture and Other Cruel Inhuman or Degrading Treatment or Punishment* was adopted by the General Assembly of the United Nations on 10 December 1984 and came in force on 26 June 1987. State Parties to the Convention desire to make more effective the struggle against torture and other cruel, inhuman or degrading treatment or punishment throughout the world.

- *The Convention on the Rights of the Child* came into force in 2 September 1990 less than one year after it had been adopted by the United Nations General Assembly on 20 November 1989. States Parties to the Convention agree to take all appropriate measures to implement the rights recognized in the Convention, and in doing so the best interest of the child shall be the paramount consideration and guiding principle. The provisions are wide - ranging and include recognition of the importance of family life for the Child. The United Nations Children's Fund (UNICEF)[9], which plays an important role in promoting the Convention, is a significant participant in these proceedings.

- *The Declaration on the Rights of Persons Belonging to National or Ethnic, Religious and Linguistic Minorities* is the most comprehensive United Nations human rights instrument devoted solely to minority rights. It was adopted by consensus by the United Nations General Assembly in 1992[10]. The Preamble to the Declaration states that the promotion and realization of the rights of persons belonging to minorities is an 'integral part of the development of society… within a democratic frame work based on the rule of law….' Article 1 of the Declaration requires States to recognize and promote the identity of such minorities.

- The main international instrument to protect the rights of the indigenous people is the *International Labour Organization Convention No. 169* concerning Indigenous and Tribal Peoples in Independent Countries. It was adopted in June 1989 and came into force in September 1991. It affirms that no State or social group has the right to deny the identity of indigenous peoples, and places responsibility on States for ensuring, with the participation of indigenous peoples, their rights and integrity. *The United Nations Working Group on Indigenous Populations,* created in 1982, is the centre of indigenous rights activities within the United Nations system.
- The Human Rights of the Refugees is protected by the Convention relating to the Status of Refugees (1951) and its Protocol (1966). *The Office of the United Nations High Commissioner for Refugees* (UNHCR) is responsible for supervising international provisions for the protection of refugees and for seeking durable solutions by assisting governments to facilitate the voluntary repatriation of refugees and/or their integration within new national communities.

High Commissioner for Human Rights: Role and Functions

The Vienna Declaration and Programme of Action (1993) recognized the need for adopting the United Nations machinery for the promotion and protection of human rights to current and future needs and recommended considering the establishment of a High Commissioner for Human Rights[11]. This was achieved on 20 December 1993 when the United Nations General Assembly unanimously adopted Resolution 48/141 establishing the post of the *High Commissioner for the Promotion and Protection of all Human Rights.*

The High Commissioner for Human Rights, appointed for four years with the possibility of one renewal, must function within the framework of the United Nations Charter, the Universal Declaration of Human Rights and other relevant instruments to promote universal respect for observance of all human rights, and must be guided by the recognition that 'all human rights - civil, cultural, economic, political and social - are universal, indivisible, interdependent and interrelated', and the promotion and protection of human rights is the legitimate concern of the international community. The principal responsibilities of the High Commissioner are as follows:

- Co-ordinating human rights promotion and protection activities throughout the United Nations system;
- Providing advisory services and technical and financial assistance through the Centre for Human Rights;
- Rationalization, adoption, strengthening and streamlining of the United Nations human rights machinery;
- Engaging in dialogue with all governments with a view to securing respect for all human rights; and
- Playing an active role in preventing the continuation of human rights violations throughout the world.

The United Nations Centre for Human Rights serves as a focal point for United Nations activities in the field of human rights. It was created in 1982 by Resolution 37/437 of the General Assembly by the redesignation of the former Division of Human Rights. The Centre, which is located in Geneva with an office in New York, is headed by an Assistant Secretary - General.

The main functions of the Centre are to assist United Nations organs and bodies in the promotion and protection of human rights and fundamental freedoms as envisaged by the Charter of the United nations, the Universal Declaration of Human Rights and the International Covenants on Human Rights and in resolutions of the General Assembly.

Individual Nation States Verses International Scrutiny of Compliance of Human Rights has emerged as a much debated issue in modern times. The State is the guarantor and protector of human rights, and according to customary rule regulating the relations between states, governments in principle have no right to intervene in the internal affairs of another State. For a long time human rights were understood as being a State's internal responsibility. This understanding began to be eroded by the realization that human rights violations present a threat to peace and security in the world. In 1993, the Vienna Declaration and Programme of Action, adopted by the World Conference on Human Rights, stated that 'the promotion and protection of all human rights is a legitimate concern of the international community' (Article 4). Like wise, in Resolution 48/125 of 20 December 1993, in paragraphs 3 and 5 of the operative part, the United Nations General Assembly reaffirmed that it is 'a purpose of the United Nations and the task of all Member States... to promote and encourage respect for human rights and fundamental freedoms and to remain vigilant with regard to violations of human rights wherever they occur'. It also confirmed that 'the promotion, protection and full realization of all human rights and fundamental freedoms, as legitimate concerns of the world community, should be guided by the principles of non-selectivity, impartiality and objectivity'.

States usually remain sensitive and defensive regarding the scrutiny of their human rights records and continue to invoke Article 2(7) of the United Nations Charter, which stipulates that the United Nations should not intervene 'in matters, which are essentially within the domestic jurisdiction of any state'. However, such behaviour is increasingly recognized as being an attempt not to fulfil the obligations under international law. The United Nations Charter recognizes that peace and stability among nations is related to the recognition of and respect for human rights, and seeks to establish conditions under which both peace and human rights, which include the social and economic advancement of all people, can be achieved.

POINTS TO REMEMBER

- Since the end of the First World War, there has been a growing belief that governments alone cannot safeguard human rights. International instruments were needed to codify and protect human rights. This conviction was reflected in and reinforced by the Charter of the United Nations signed on 20 June 1945.
- The Universal Declaration of Human Rights was approved by the General Assembly of the United Nations on December 10, 1948. It provided the basis for the formulation by the United Nations of Covenant and Conventions, Declarations and Recommendations on specific issues.
- Three documents - the Universal Declaration of Human Rights, the International Covenant on Civil and Political Rights, and the

International Covenant on Economic, Social and Cultural rights along with two protocols constitute the International Bill of Human Rights.

- Although the Universal Declaration of Human Rights is not legally binding, it has become a common reference in human rights for all nations.
- Besides the International Bill of Human Rights, there are a large number of conventions, declarations and recommendations adopted by the General Assembly and other legislative bodies of the United Nations system, which elaborate on Human Rights.
- The post of the High Commissioner of Human Rights was created in 1993 for the Promotion and protection of all Human Rights.
- International scrutiny in regard to compliance of Human Rights by individual nations does not amount interference in internal affairs.

NOTES AND REFERENCES

1. For details see Arjun Dev.et al .,(ed.) (1996) *Human Rights; A Source Book,* New Delhi, NCERT. As the title suggests, the book provides a bird's eye view of the subject. It provides useful information on the various efforts, which have been made by the world community particularly the UN in the direction of Human Rights..
2. For comprehensive analysis of UDHR, see *Basic Facts About the United Nations* (1994), Department of Public Information, United Nations, New York, pp. 151 - 153.
3. *Ibid.*
4. *Ibid.*, p.151.
5. *Ibid.*, p. 153.
6. As on 1 January 1996, there were 185 Member states of the United Nations.
7. No. 2, p.153.
8. Adopted by Resolution 48/104 of 20 December 1993.
9. UNICEF was awarded the Nobel Peace Prize in 1965.
10. Adopted by Resolution 47/235 of 18 December 1992.
11. Vienna Declaration and Programme of Action, Para. 18.

SUGGESTED READING

1. Arjun Dev, Indira Arjun Dev, Supta Dev (eds.) (1996) *Human Rights: A Source Book,* NCERT, New Delhi.
2. *Basic Facts About the United Nations* (1994), Department of Public Information, United Nations, New York.

3. *Birthright of Man (1969)*UNESCO, Paris.
4. James Fawcett (1985) *Social Science Encyclopedia,* Routledge, New York.
5. P. Alston (ed.), (1992) *The United Nations and Human Rights: A Critical Approach,* Clarendon Press, Oxford.

MODEL QUESTIONS

Objective Questions (2 Mark Each)

1. The first international treaties concerning human rights centered around which issues?
2. Which articles of the UN Charter pledge to protect Human Rights?
3. Which body was assigned the task of drawing up an International Bill of Human Rights.
4. When was the Universal Declaration of Human Rights adopted?

Short Questions (5 Marks Each)

1. What are the categories of rights proclaimed in the Universal Declaration of Human Rights?
2. Briefly discuss functions of the High Commissioner of Human Rights.

Long Questions (15 Marks Each)

1. Critically discuss the significance of the Universal Declaration of Human Rights.
2. What other important United Nations Human Rights instruments exist besides the International Bill of Human Rights?

4

INDIAN PERSPECTIVE ON HUMAN RIGHTS

Human Rights in the Indian Tradition

The quest for equilibrium, harmony, knowledge and truth has been an integral part of the Indian tradition since times immemorial. More than five thousand years ago, the ancient Indian philosophers and thinkers expounded a theory of higher moral law over and above positive law embodying values of universal validity, the aim of which was to establish a harmonious social order by striking a balance between spiritual and material aspects of life. It was the concept of *Dharma* which governed in an integrative manner all civil, religious and other actions of men in society be it king or his subjects. The *Law of Dharma* in ancient India made a bold attempt at building an organized social life wherein each individual realized his goals within the parameters of social norms of morality. The *Natural Law* so revealed in the *Vedas, Puranas*, and the epics *Ramayana* and *Mahabharata* was extolled by the mystics, saints, philosophers and poets of the time. The philosophy expounded by the saints of ancient India was a reinstatement of Natural Law with religious fervour to enthuse people towards the path of enlightenment and unity.

Ancient Indians were not indifferent or unaware of human rights jurisprudence. The basis of ancient human rights jurisprudence was *Dharma* which aimed at the establishment of a socio - legal order free from traces of conflicts, exploitation and miseries. The root of the concern for human rights in the Vedic era may be traced to religion. Theology presented the basis for a human rights philosophy stemming from a law higher than the state, the source of which was traced to the supreme being. It was believed that as human beings were created in the image of God they were endowed with intrinsic worth and dignity. The components of comprehensive human rights jurisprudence thus logically emerged from this premise. The philosophers of the Vedic age believed that human rights were based on mankind's increasing demand for life in which the inherent dignity and worth of each human being deserved to receive respect and protection. The prime importance of human rights was aptly summed up in the rich Indian legacy of "*Vashudhaiva - Kutumbakam*" or "We are all human family". References occur as early as in the *Rigveda* to the three Civil Rights, that of *Tana (body), Skridhi (dwelling place)* and *Jibhasi (life).*

Panini, the great Sanskrit grammarian of the 5th century B.C. interpreted *Dharma* as an act of religious merit, custom and usage. According to him, it was the duty of the king to protect his subjects against disorder and anarchy. The ancient lawgiver *Manu* laid down elaborate rules for the guidance of the king. It was his duty to uphold the law, and he was as much subject to law as any other person. It was obligatory upon the king to enforce not only the sacred law of the texts but also the customary laws relating to the rights and claims of the subjects. *Kautilya,* the author of the famous political treatise *Arthasastra* (4th century B.C) not only affirmed and elaborated the civil and legal rights of citizens but also added a number of economic rights. He categorically ordained the king to provide for the orphan, the aged and infirm besides providing subsistence to helpless expectant mothers and their children. According to Kautilya, the king's function was not only conceived in terms of legislation but also protection which involved protection of the subjects not only from invasion but also the protection of the order of the society. The *Mahabharata* also propagates revolt against an oppressive ruler. Even killing of such a king was allowed in exceptional circumstances. The Tamil epic *Tirukkural* by *Truvullauvar* narrates in detail the inherent civil, political, economic, social and cultural rights of the individual.

The rise of *Buddhism (Sixth Century BC)* and *Jainism (Sixth Century BC)* in the post - Vedic period was a reaction to the downfall of Human Rights jurisprudence. These traditions with their emphasis on the values of egalitarianism hit at the very roots of the caste system. *Ashoka the Great* carried forward the legacy of the Buddhist traditions and successfully established a welfare state. The golden era of the Guptas (300 to 500 AD) followed by the Vardhan dynasty as evident from the accounts of Chinese travelers Fahein and Hieuen Tsang respectively vividly describe the commitment of the rulers to *Rajyadharma.*

The Islamic traditions of human rights jurisprudence became evident in the medieval ages. Being inspired by the tenets of the Holy Koran it preached universal brotherhood, justice, compassion and equality. Its finest manifestation was in the era of *Akbar the Great* (1555-1606). The Mughal emperor Akbar, with his policy of universal reconciliation and tolerance inaugurated an era of healthy traditions in statecraft. His justice - loving tradition was followed by his son Jehangir. The *Bhakti* and the *Sufi* traditions too in their own unique ways popularized the idea of universal brotherhood. It revived and regenerated the cherished Indian values of truth, righteousness, justice and morality. These values were rooted in religion, humanitarian traditions and the unceasing struggle for freedom and equality.

The philosophy of human rights in the modern sense took shape during the course of British rule. Resistance to foreign rule was manifested in the form of demand for fundamental freedoms and civil and political rights for the people of India. The concrete demand for fundamental rights came logically in the wake of the Nationalist Movement which coincided with the birth of the Indian National Congress in 1885. The first explicit demand of the people of the Indian sub-continent for fundamental rights found place in the *Constitution of India Bill, 1895*, also known as the *'Home Rule Document'*. This bill emphasized on the formulation of a Constitution which would guarantee every citizen basic human rights of life and liberty. It was in 1925 that the Indian National Congress finalized a draft of the "Commonwealth of India Bill" which embodied in it a Declaration of Rights, the demand for which was vehemently repeated by the Motilal Nehru Committee appointed in 1928. The *Karachi Session of Congress in 1931* adopted a detailed programme on fundamental rights with the demand for it to be included in the *Government of India Act 1935.* In 1945, the Tej Bahadur Sapru Committee stressed on the need for a written code of fundamental rights. The result was the forceful demand of the Constituent Assembly to include human rights in the Constitution of Independent India. The promulgation of the Constitution of Independent India, by the people of India in January 1950, is a watershed in the history of India. *The Preamble, Fundamental Rights* and the *Directive Principles of State Policy* together provide the basic Human Rights for the people of India.

Human Rights and the Indian Constitution: Constitutional and Legal Framework

Broadly speaking, Human Rights provisions in India may be divided into two broad categories which are as follows:

- Constitutional Provisions (Constitutional Framework)
- Statutory Provisions (Legal Framework)

The Constitutional Provisions of Human Rights are those provisions which arise from the constitution itself. In the Constitution of India, there are certain very important Human Rights provisions. These are: *The Preamble; Part III Fundamental Rights; Part IV Directive Principles of State Policy, Part IVA of the Constitution on Fundamental Duties* and Articles *226, 300A, 325* and *326*[1].

These provisions together reflect the basic principles of the *Universal Declaration of Human Rights* and the *Covenants on Civil and Political Rights*, and *Economic, Social and Cultural Rights.*

The Preamble of the Indian Constitution has set forth the basic objectives to be achieved by the Constitution. It may be read as under: *We, The People of India,* having solemnly resolved to constitute India into a *Sovereign Socialist Secular Democratic Republic* and to secure to all its citizens:

Justice, social, economic, and political;
Liberty of thought, expression, belief, faith and worship;
Equality of status and of opportunity; and to promote among them all;
Fraternity assuring the dignity of the individual and the unity and integrity of the Nation;

In Our Constituent Assembly this twenty sixth day of November 1949, do *hereby adopt, enact and give to ourselves this Constitution.*

The Preamble itself is very clear. Human Rights may be regarded to be the offspring of the Preamble.

Part III of the Indian Constitution deals with the *Fundamental Rights.* Human Rights as enumerated in the Constitution as Fundamental Rights are as follows:

Right to Equality (Articles 14 - 18)

y before Law.

- Prohibition of discrimination on grounds of religion, race, caste, sex or place of birth.
- Equality of opportunity in matters of public employment
- Abolition of Untouchability.
- Abolition of Titles.

- **Right to Freedom (Articles 19 - 22)**
  - *Protection of certain rights pertaining to freedom.*
  - Protection in respect of conviction for offences.
  - Protection of life and personal liberty.
  - Protection against arrest and detention in certain cases.

- **Right Against Exploitation (Articles 23 - 24)**
  - Prohibition of traffic in human beings and forced labour.
  - Prohibition of employment of children in factories etc.

- **Right to Freedom of Religion (Articles 25 - 28)**
  - Freedom of conscience and free profession, practice and propagation of religion.
  - Freedom to manage religious affairs.
  - Freedom as to payment of taxes for promotion of any particular religion.
  - Freedom as to attendance at religious instruction or religious worship in certain educational institutions.

- **Cultural and Educational Rights (Articles 29 - 31)**
  - Protection of interests of minorities
  - Right of minorities to establish and administer educational institutions.
  - *Saving of laws giving effect to certain directive principles.*

- **Right to Constitutional Remedies (Article 32 - 34)**

The citizens of India have four distinct kind of rights, which can be classified as (i) *Rights (ii) Liberties (iii) Power and (iv) Immunities.*

The Directive Principles of State Policy are included *in Part IV* of the Indian Constitution (*Articles 36 - 51).* The first three Articles (36, 37 and 38) of the Chapter on Directive Principles are general in character and deal with definitions, legal effects and objectives. The remaining articles may be grouped into three distinct categories[2]:

(i) those that aim to shape India into a welfare state;

(ii) those that aim to shape India into a Gandhian state; and

(iii) those that aim to promote international peace.

A detailed study is as follows:

(i) *Article 38* provides that the state shall promote the welfare of the people by securing and protecting as effectively as it may a social order in which justice - social, economic and political shall inform all the institutions of national life. Thus promotion and the welfare of the people is the objective which the Constitution sets forth. *Article 39*, then, proceeds to spell out the methods by which the object of general welfare, through justice, can be obtained and the basis of a new social order established. With this end in view, the state shall direct its policy in securing:

- adequate means of livelihood for all citizens, men and women equally;
- distribution of wealth so as to serve the common people;
- equal pay for equal work for both men and women;
- protection of child and youth against exploitation against moral and material abandonment;
- provision of work and education for all people, relief in case of unemployment, old age, sickness and disablement;
- just and human conditions of work and maternity relief;
- free and compulsory education for all children until they reach the age of fourteen years; and
- raising the level of nutrition and the standard of living and the improvement of public health.

(ii) Some of the Directive Principles are in accordance with and conform to the Gandhian ways of life and fulfil the requirements of a predominantly non-violent state of Gandhi's conception. These principles enjoin that;

- the state shall take steps to organize village panchayats and endow them with such power and authority as may be necessary to enable them to function as units of self governance;
- the state shall endeavor to promote cottage industries on an individual or co-operative basis in rural areas;
- the state shall promote with special care the educational and economic interest of the weaker sections of the people and in particular, of the Scheduled Castes and the Scheduled Tribes in order to protect them from social injustice and all forms of exploitation;
- the state shall bring about prohibition of the consumption, except for medicinal purpose, of intoxicating drinks and of drugs which are injurious to health;
- the state shall organize agriculture and animal husbandry on modern and scientific lines;
- the state shall take steps for preserving and improving the breeds, and prohibiting the slaughter of cows and calves and other milch cattle;
- the state shall protect, preserve and maintain places of national and historical importance; and
- the state shall take steps to separate the judiciary from the executive; and secure for citizens a uniform civil code throughout the country.

(iii) In the International field India shall strive:

- to promote international peace and security;
- to maintain just and honourable relations between nations;
- to foster respect for international law and treaty obligations; and
- to encourage settlement of international disputes by arbitration.

The founding fathers of the Indian Constitution hoped that through the Directive Principles of State Policy, Human Rights would be protected and preserved.

It is being increasingly recognized that rights and duties go hand in hand. In the Indian Constitution, Fundamental Rights are complimented by *Fundamental Duties. Part IVA* of the Indian Constitution lays down fundamental duties for the citizen of India[3]. *Article 51A* states that it shall be the duty of every citizen of India:

- to abide by the Constitution and respect its ideals and institutions, the National Flag and the National Anthem;
- to cherish and follow the noble ideals which inspired our national struggle for freedom;
- to uphold and protect the sovereignty, unity and integrity of India;
- to defend the country and render national service when called upon to do so;
- to promote harmony and the spirit of common brotherhood amongst all the people of India transcending religious, linguistic and regional or sectional diversities; to renounce practices derogatory to the dignity of women;
- to value and preserve the rich heritage of our composite culture;
- to protect and improve the natural environment including forests, lakes, rivers and wild life, and to have compassion for living creatures;
- to develop the scientific temper, humanism and the spirit of inquiry and reform;
- to safeguard public property and to abjure violence; and
- to strive towards excellence in all spheres of individual and collective activity so that the nation constantly rises to higher levels of endeavour and achievement.

There are some *other Constitutional Provisions* which have a direct bearing on Human Rights protection. These are:

- *Article 226* which concerns the power of the High Courts to issue certain writs like *habeas corpus, mandamus, prohibition, quo warranto and certiorari.*

- *Article 300A* which states that no person shall be deprived of his property save by authority of law.
- *Article 325* which states that no person shall be ineligible for inclusion in, or claim to be included in a special, electoral roll on grounds of religion, race, caste or sex.
- *Article 326* which states that elections to the House of People and to the Legislative Assemblies of States will be on the basis of adult suffrage.

The Statutory Provisions on Human Rights are those provisions, which have been derived from various enactments of Central and State governments. Some such important provisions are[4]:

- Protection of Human Rights Act, 1993.
- National Commission for Scheduled Castes and Scheduled Tribes.
- National Commission for Minorities Act, 1992.
- National Commission for Women Act, 1990.
- Protection of Civil Rights Act, 1955.
- Scheduled Castes and Scheduled Tribes (Prevention of Atrocities) Act, 1989.
- Immoral Traffic (Prevention) Act 1956.
- Indecent Representation of Women (Prohibition) Act, 1986.
- Dowry Prohibition Act, 1961.
- Commission of Sati (Prevention) Act, 1987.
- Maternity Benefit Act, 1961.
- Child Marriage Restraint Act, 1929.
- Children Act, 1960.
- Child Labour (Prohibition and Regulation) Act, 1986.
- Caste Disabilities Removal Act, 1950.
- Mental Health Act, 1987.
- Bonded Labour (System) Abolition Act, 1976.

Human Rights violation can thus be grouped under two categories. Firstly, violations by the state and its agencies. Secondly, violations that occur in the domain of civil society on account of undemocratic social structures. It is only through a multi-pronged approach that the issue of violation of Human Rights can be addressed.

Human Rights Enforcement: Human Rights Commissions and Special Commissions for Weaker Sections

Human rights enforcement is key to human rights protection. This calls for effective enforcement agencies. In this direction some significant acts have been passed by the Indian Parliament from time to time which has resulted in the constitution of Special Commissions like the *Human Rights Commissions, Special Commission for Scheduled Caste and Scheduled Tribes, National Commission for Women and the National Commission for Minorities.*

National Human Rights Commission (NHRC)

The National Human Rights Commission was constituted in October 1993 under the Human Rights Ordinance of 28 September 1993, which was soon after enacted as the *Protection of Human Rights Act, 1993*[5]. It is fully an autonomous body, its autonomy derived out of the method of appointment of its members and the statutory guarantees thereto besides the autonomy it enjoys in terms of its financial powers.

The Commission shall consist of:

- a Chairperson who has been a Chief Justice of the Supreme Court;
- one Member who is or has been the Chief Justice of a Supreme Court;
- one Member who is, or has been, the Chief Justice of a High Court; and
- two Members to be appointed from amongst persons having knowledge of, or practical experience in, matters relating to human rights.

The Chairperson of the National Commission for Minorities, the National Commission for the Scheduled Castes and Scheduled Tribes and the National Commission for Women shall be deemed to be Members of the Commission for the discharge of certain functions.

There shall be a Secretary General of the rank of the Secretary to the Government of India who shall function as the Chief Executive Officer of the Commission.

The Chairperson and other members of the Commission are appointed by the *President of India* on the recommendations of a high - powered Committee consisting of the *Prime Minister, Speaker of the House of People, Leader of the Opposition in the House of People, Leader of the Opposition in the Council of States* and *Deputy Chairman of the Council of States*

The term of office of the Chairperson and members will be five years from the date of assumption of office or until the age of 70 years, whichever is earlier. The Chairperson or any other Member of the Commission can only be removed from his office by an order of the President on the ground of proved misbehaviour or incapacity.

The Headquarters of the Commission shall be at New Delhi. However, there is an enabling provision in the Act to establish offices at other places in India with the previous approval of the Central Government.

Powers and Functions of the NHRC

The NHRC enjoys all the powers of a civil court under the code of civil procedure. It sends summons to the concerned persons, enforces the attendance of witnesses and examines them on oath. It has the power of receiving evidence on affidavits. It can ask for any public record or copy thereof from any office or court to carry on its inquiry. The Commission may enter any place of office where the Commission has the reason to believe that any document relating to the subject matter of inquiry may be found. The following functions devolve on the Commission under the Act.

- To inquire, on its own initiative or on a petition presented to it by a victim into complaints of violation of human rights or negligence in the prevention of such violation by a public servant;
- Intervene in any proceeding involving any allegation of violation of human rights pending before a court with approval of such court;
- Review the factors, including acts of terrorism that inhibit the enjoyment of human rights and recommend appropriate remedial measures;
- Review the safeguards provided by or under the Constitution or any law for the time being in force for the protection of human rights and recommend measures for their effective implementation;

- Strive to create awareness among the people in society by spreading human rights literacy among various sections of society and promote awareness of safeguards available for the protection of these rights through publications, the media, seminars and other available means;
- Encourage the efforts of non-governmental organizations and institutions working in the field of human rights;
- Visit, under intimation to the State government, any institution under the control of the State Government, where persons are detained or lodged for purposes of treatment, reformation or protection ,to study the living conditions of the inmates and make recommendations thereon;
- Study treaties and other international instruments on human rights and make recommendations for their effective implementation;
- Undertake and promote research in the field of human rights; and
- Promote such activities as it may consider necessary for the promotion of human rights

The Commission is required to submit an *Annual Report* to the Central Government as well as the State Governments concerned. Besides, the Commission may at any time submit *Special Reports* on any matter which, in its opinion, is of such urgency or importance that it should not be deferred till submission of the Annual Report. It is enjoined on the Central Government as well as the concerned State Government to lay before each House of Parliament or the State Legislatures respectively the Annual and Special Reports of the Commission along with a memorandum of action taken or proposed to be taken on the recommendations of the Commission and the reasons for non-acceptance of the recommendations, if any.

It is beyond doubt that *Human Rights education* is crucial for the fulfillment of the commitment made in the Constitution of India. There is an assumption that lack of information on human rights literacy is the source of human rights violation. Therefore section 12(h) of the Protection of Human Rights Act 1993 specifically states that NHRC should spread human rights literacy among various sections of society. This is sought to be done by seminars, publications and other available means. In this direction, the NHRC has identified three important sectors of the Indian society: (i) *The Political Parties* (ii) *The Executive authority at all levels and* (iii) *Educationists.* It is the observation of the NHRC that the political parties of the country by their behaviour and ideals can become the most powerful forces for the protection and promotion of human rights.

In educational matters, the NHRC has initiated steps along with the *Department of Education, Ministry of Human Resource Development and the National Council for Educational Research and Training (NCERT),* for evolving appropriately graded curricula for various levels of schooling. The Commission has addressed communications to all vice-chancellors of different Universities of India proposing four measures.

- that the subject of human rights may find a place in the curriculum of the University.
- that research, seminars and publications conserving human rights should be furthered.
- that the Commission would encourage linkages between the academic community and non-governmental organizations.
- that the Commission would welcome continuing contact with the Universities in these areas and would give all help within its means and possibilities.

The NHRC has also encouraged other training institutions to impart human rights education. The Sardar Vallabh Bhai Patel National Academy in Hyderabad has included the teaching of human rights in its courses at the initiative of the Commission. At the state level too, there are increasing instances of police training institutes focussing on this key aspect of professional training.

State Human Rights Commissions

There is an enabling provision in the *Protection of Human Rights Act 1993,* for State Human Rights Commission to be constituted by the respective State Governments[6]. The state Commission shall consist of:

- a Chairperson who has been a Chief Justice of a High Court;
- one Member who is, or has been a Judge of a High Court;
- one Member who is, or has been, a District Judge in that State;
- two Members to be appointed from amongst persons having knowledge of, or practical experience in, matters relating to human rights.

The Chairperson and other Members of the Commission shall be appointed by the Government after obtaining the recommendations of a Committee consisting of the *Chief Minister, Speaker of the Legislative Assembly, Minister-in-charge of the Department of Home in that State* and the *Leader of the Opposition in the Legislative Assembly.*

The term of office of the Chairperson or Member will be five years from the date of assumption of office. The Chairperson or any other Member of a State Commission can only be removed by the President of India in accordance with the procedure envisaged for the National Commission. There shall be a secretary who shall be the Chief Executive Officer of the State Commission and shall exercise such powers and discharge such functions of the State Commission as it may delegate to him.

The headquarters of the State Commission shall be at such place as the State Government may by notification, specify.

A State Commission may inquire into violations of human rights only in respect of matters relating to any of the entries enumerated in List II (State List) and List III (Concurrent List) in the Seventh Schedule of the Constitution. However, if any such matter is already being inquired into by the National Commission or any other Statutory Commission, the State Commission shall not inquire into the said matter. Subject to this, the powers, the procedures of investigation, inquiry and steps to be taken there after are comparable to those of the National Commission.

The State Commission shall submit *Annual Report* to the respective State Governments and may, at any time, submit Special Reports on any matter which in their opinion is of urgency or importance. It is enjoined on the State Governments to cause to lay on the table of the respective State Legislature, the Annual and Special Reports of the State Human Rights Commission.

Special *Human Rights Courts* may be constituted for the purpose of providing speedy trial of offences arising out of violations of human rights. The State Governments may with the concurrence of the Chief Justice of the concerned High Court specify for each District Court of Sessions to be a Human Rights Court to try such offences.

National Commission for Scheduled Caste and Scheduled Tribes:

In 1989 the *Scheduled Caste and the Scheduled Tribes* Act was passed (prevention of atrocities), to constitute a *National Commission for Scheduled Caste and Scheduled Tribes*[7]. The Commission consists of a Chairperson, Vice-Chairperson and five other members. All of them are appointed by the President of India.

The Commission shall have the power to regulate its own procedure. It shall be the duty of the Commission:

- to investigate and monitor all matters relating to the safeguards provided for the scheduled caste and scheduled tribes under this Commission.
- to enquire into specific complains with respect to the deprivation of rights and safeguards of the scheduled caste and scheduled tribes.
- to participate and advise on the planning process of socio-economic development of the scheduled caste and scheduled tribes and to evaluate the progress of that development under the union and any state.
- to present to the president annually and at such other times as the Commission may deem fit, reports upon the working of those safeguards.
- to discharge such other functions in relations to the protection, welfare, development and advancement of the scheduled caste and scheduled tribes.

The commission while investigating any matter shall have all the powers of a civil court trying a suit and in particular in respect of the following matters, namely:

- summoning and enforcing the attendance of any person from any part of India and examining him on oath.
- requiring the discovery and production of any documents.
- receiving evidence on affidavits.
- requisitioning any public record or copy thereof from any court or office.
- issuing commissions for the examination of witnesses and documents; and
- any other matter which the President may by rule determine.

The Union and every state government shall consult the Commission on all major policy matters affecting Scheduled Caste and Scheduled Tribes.

National Commission for Women

In 1990 the *National Commission for Women Act* was passed in the Parliament to constitute a National Commission for Women[8]. The Commission consists of:

- A Chairperson, to be nominated by the Central Government.
- Five members to the nominated by the Central Government from amongs persons who have had experience in legislation, trade unionism, management of an industry etc.
- A member secretary to be nominated by the Central Government.

The term of office and condition of service of Chairperson and members are as follows:

- Chairperson and every Member shall hold office for a period not exceeding three years or as may be specified by the central government.
- The Chairperson or a member may resign from office of Chairperson or as the case may be of the member at any time.
- The Central Government shall remove a person from the office of Chairperson or member if the person gets convicted and sentenced to imprisonment for an offence.
- Becomes bankrupt.
- Refuses to act or becomes incapable of performing his/her duties.

The salary and allowances payable to and the other terms and condition of service of the Chairperson and members shall be such as may be prescribed.

The Commission shall perform all or any of the following functions, namely -

- investigate and examine all matters relating to the safeguards provided for women under the Constitution and other laws.
- present to the Central Government annually the reports upon the working of those safeguards.

- make recommendations for the effective implementation of those safeguards for improving the conditions of women by the union or any state.
- review, for time to time the existing provisions of the Constitution and other laws affecting women.
- take up the cases of violation of the provisions of the Constitution and of other laws relating to women with the appropriate authority.
- call for special investigation into specific situation arising out of discrimination and atrocities against women.
- undertake promotional and educational research so as to suggest ways of ensuring due representation of women in all spheres and identify factors responsible for obstructing their advancement.
- participate and advice on the planning process of socio-economic development of women.
- evaluate the progress of development of women under the union and any state.
- inspect a jail, remand home, women institution or other place of custody where women are kept as prisoners, and take up with the concerned authorities for remedial action, if found necessary.
- fund litigation involving issues affecting a large body of women.
- make periodical reports to the government on any matter pertaining to women.
- any other matter which may be referred to it by the Central Government.

National Commission for Minorities

In 1992 the *National Commission for Minorities Act was* passed in the Parliament to constitute a National Commission for Minorities[9]. The Commission consists of a Chairperson, a Vice-chairperson and five members to be nominated by the Central Government. The Chairperson and five members shall be from among the minority communities.

The term of office and condition of service of Chairperson and members are such:

- The Chairperson and every member shall hold office for a term of three year from the date he/she assumes office.

- The Chairperson or a member may resign from the office of Chairperson or, as the case may be, of the member at any time.
- The Central Government shall remove a person from the office of Chairperson or a member if that person is convicted and sentenced to imprisonment for an offence..
- Becomes of unsound mind.
- Refuses to act or becomes incapable of acting.
- Is absent from there consecutive meetings of theCommission.
- The salaries and allowance payable to and other terms and condition of the service of the Chairperson and members shall be such as may be prescribed.

Functions of the Commission

The Commission shall perform all or any of the following functions namely:

- Evaluate the progress of the development of minorities under the union and state.
- Monitor the working for the safeguards provided in the Constitution and in laws enacted by the Parliament and the state legislative assemblies.
- Make recommendations for the effective implementation of safeguards for the protection of the interest of minorities by the Central Government and the State Government.
- Look into specific complains regarding deprivation of rights and safeguard of the minorities and take up such matters with the appropriate authorities.
- Conduct studies, research and analysis on the issues relating to socio-economic and educational development of minorities.
- Suggest appropriate measures in respect of any minority to be undertaken by the Central Government or the State Governments.
- Make periodical or special reports to the Central Governments on any matter pertaining to minorities and in particular to difficulties confronted by them; and
- Any other matter which may be referred to it by the Central Government.

Thus, it is evident that through various statutory provisions derived from various enactment of Central and State Governments, serious attempts have been made to protect and promote respect for human rights.

Human Rights Education: UNESCO and Montreal Protocol

The effective implementation of human rights demands that people be aware of their own rights and of those of others, so as to be able to demand their implementation and protection. Knowledge of human rights and of ways to protect them is an indispensable precondition to ensure that these rights are not disregarded. In view of the importance of information about human rights, the United Nations General Assembly adopted several resolutions. On 10 December 1988, a *United Nations World Public Information Campaign for Human Rights* was launched by General Assembly Resolution 43/128. The aim of this campaign was to develop programmes of teaching, education and information in the field of human rights in a global and practically oriented fashion. The need for clear and accessible information on human rights, tailored to regional and national requirements and disseminated by national and local languages was acknowledged. Member states were urged to include in their education curricula materials relevant to a comprehensive understanding of human rights issues, and all those responsible for training law - enforcement officials, members of the armed forces, medical personnel and diplomats were encouraged to include appropriate human rights components in their programmes. Every two years the Secretary -General presents a report on the campaign activities which include the production and dissemination of printed material on human rights, the organization of workshops and seminars, the granting of fellowships and the creation of national human rights institutions. *The United Nations Centre for Human Rights* co-ordinates the activities of the world campaign within the United Nations system and also discusses with governments, regional and national institutions and interested individuals in the development and implementation of various human rights activities.

UNESCO and Human Rights Education

The United Nations Educational, Scientific and Cultural Organization (UNESCO) came into existence on November 4, 1946. It is one of the recognized specialized agencies of the United Nations. UNESCO's competence extends to the rights relating to *education, science (including social science), and culture and communications,* which includes freedom of opinion and expression, and freedom of the press.

UNESCO, in accordance with its Constitution, adopted in 1945, should 'contribute to peace and security by promoting collaboration among the nations through education, science and culture in order to further universal respect for justice, for the rule of law and for human rights and fundamental freedoms' (Article 26). Guided by the Universal Declaration of Human Rights, UNESCO has made efforts to develop its provisions by condifying certain rights within its field of competence and to disseminate knowledge on human rights by means of education.

The UNESCO Convention against Discrimination in Education entered into force in 1962. More than eighty states have become parties to it[10]. This Convention commits states parties to a national policy which will promote equality of opportunity and treatment in matters of education. States Parties undertake to ensure, by legislation if required that there is no discrimination in the admission of pupils to educational institutions, nor any discrimination in the treatment of students. Foreign nationals are assured of the same access to education. The measures for implementation are based on a system of reports from the participating states which are examined by a special *Committee on Convention and Recommendations.* The report and comments of the committee are then submitted to the General Conference of UNESCO. Other procedures exist for the implementation of other UNESCO instruments relating to such matters as the *Status of Teachers.* The joint *International Labour Organization/ UNESCO Committee of Experts on the Application of the Recommendation Concerning the Status of Teachers was set up in 1968.*

UNESCO has also undertaken efforts to protect cultural property, considering that this field of interest is closely linked with cultural rights. There are three UNESCO Conventions: the *Convention for the Protection of Cultural Property in the Event of Armed Conflict* (the 'Hague' Convention), with Regulations for the Execution of the Convention, as well as the Protocol to the Convention and the Conference Resolutions (1954); the *Convention on the Means of Prohibiting and Preventing the Illicit Import, Export and Transfer of Ownership of Cultural Property (1970); and the Convention Concerning the Protection of the World Cultural and Natural Heritage.*

UNESCO has also undertaken numerous activities in order to further develop the right to participate in cultural life. *The Declaration of the Principles of International Cultural Co-operation* (1966) stresses that international Co-operation should 'enable everyone to have access to knowledge, to enjoy the arts and literature of all peoples, to share in advances made in science in all parts of the world and in resulting benefits, and to contribute to the enrichment of cultural life' (Article IV, para. 4). *The Recommendation by the People at Large in Cultural Life and Their Contribution to it (1976)* defines access to culture as opportunities available for everyone for obtaining information, training and knowledge, and for enjoying cultural values, in particular through the creation of appropriate socio-economic conditions.

A number of instruments protecting the rights of persons playing an important role in cultural and scientific life have been adopted[11].

As a *Specialized Agency* responsible for education, science, including social sciences, and culture within United Nations system, UNESCO sponsors an important inter-disciplinary research programme, which seeks to determine the social, economic and cultural factors which govern the perception of rights and their implementation. An example of such research is the project on the right to privacy and the meaning of privacy for various social strata and various societies. Another area of research is the effect of technological progress on rights in the modern state. In particular, since 1989, UNESCO has been engaged in examining legislation concerning independent and pluralist media and in advising Member States on new media legislation and possible structures for editorially independent public broadcasting services. In the monitoring of the operation of law, social science research is also important in analysing real access to equality before the law and the obstacles to the implementation of human rights.

Montreal Protocol

In March 1993, UNESCO and the United Nations Centre for Human Rights, in collaboration with the Canadian Commission for UNESCO, held an *International Congress on Education for Human Rights and Democracy in Montreal, Canada.* The Congress adopted the *World Plan of Action on Education for Human Rights and Democracy.* The Plan stresses that education for democracy is an integral aspect of education for human rights and notes that education for human rights and democracy is itself a human right and a prerequisite for the realization of human rights, democracy and social justice. The Plan outlines the means by which education for human right and democracy could be made effective and comprehensive, worldwide. The main lines of action identified in the Plan include:

- identification of target groups;
- the development of appropriate curricular;
- research into education for human rights and democracy;
- the revision of school text books with the aim of eliminating stereotypes;
- the building of networks among educators;
- increasing resources for education for human rights and democracy; and
- the design of cost - effective and sustainable educational programmes.

The plan also identifies the obstacles to be overcome in the field of human rights education.

The Vienna Declaration and Programme of Action (1993), taking account of the World Plan on Education for Human Rights and Democracy, encourages States to strive to eradicate illiteracy, to include human rights, humanitarian law, democracy and the rule of law in all formal and non-formal educational curricula, and to develop programmes for ensuring the wide dissemination of public information, taking particular account of the human rights needs of women.

By Resolution 1994/51, the Commission on Human Rights requested that the General Assembly proclaim a ten year period starting from 1 January 1995 as a decade for human rights education. By its Resolution 49/184, adopted on 21 December 1994, the United Nations General Assembly proclaimed the ten-year period beginning on 1 January 1995 as the *United Nations Decade for Human Rights Education.*

The objectives of the decade (1995 - 2004) have been spelled out in the *Plan of Action.* They include:

- The assessment of needs and the formulation of effective strategies for the furtherance of human rights education at all school levels, in vocational training and formal as well as non-formal learning.

- The building and strengthening of programmes and capacities for human rights education at the international, regional, national and local levels.
- The co-ordinated development of human rights education materials.
- The strengthening of the role and capacity of the mass media in the furtherance of human rights education.
- The global dissemination of the Universal Declaration of Human Rights in the maximum possible languages and in other forms appropriate for various levels of literacy and for the disabled.

The General Assembly appealed to all governments to contribute to the implementation of the *Plan of Action* and to step up their efforts to eradicate illiteracy and to direct education towards the full development of the human personality and to the strengthening of respect for human rights and fundamental freedoms. It further urged governmental and non-governmental educational agencies to intensify their efforts to establish and implement programmes of human rights education, particularly by preparing and implementing national plans in this field. The United Nations High Commissioner for Human Rights was requested to co-ordinate the implementation of the Plan of Action. The Centre for Human Rights of the Secretariat and the Commission on Human Rights, in co-operation with Member State, other appropriate bodies and competent non-governmental organizations were asked to support its efforts.

The General Assembly called upon international, regional and national non-governmental organizations, in particular those concerned with women, labour, development and the environment, as well as all other social justice groups, human rights advocates, educators, religious organizations and the media, to increase their involvement in formal and non-formal education in human rights.

The Advisory Committee on Education for Peace, Human Rights and Democracy was established in December 1994. It is composed of twelve high-level experts representing all regions of the world. Its main objective is to encourage activities aimed at promoting education for human rights, democracy and peace at national, regional and universal levels.

Human Rights awareness through human rights education means awareness not only of the rights but also of the duties incumbent upon individuals, social groups and nations towards each other. Human Rights education, therefore, constitutes the following:

- The awareness about rights as well as the duties;
- The promotion of understanding, tolerance and respect for differences and diversities;
- Bringing about attitudinal changes and the mind - set and sensitizing the individuals, particularly the state agencies for ensuring respect for human rights of others;
- Understanding and knowledge of various forms of exploitation and availability of the methods and methodologies, instruments and mechanisms for dealing with such violations;
- Understanding of abuse and misuse of power, exposing short comings and weaknesses in law and its enforcement;
- Evolving strategies and schemes for bringing desired favourable political, economic and social changes which help in creating conducive conditions for promotion and observance of human rights.

Human rights awareness through human rights education requires building linkages and net working between individuals belonging to different age, gender, class, ethnic, religious and linguistic groups, civil society, educational institutions, political parties and institutions and agencies dealing with human rights and human rights education at the global, national and grass root levels. The role of NGO's, media and educational institution needs to be harmonized and coalesced.

POINTS TO REMEMBER

- Respect for human rights has been central to India's cultural heritage. The quest for equilibrium, harmony, knowledge and truth inspired the thinkers and philosophers of India since times immemorial. The Vedic, Jain, Buddhist and Islamic traditions in different ways contributed to the enrichment of human rights jurisprudence in India. The philosophy of human rights in the modern sense took shape during the course of the British rule in India.

- The promulgation of the Constitution of India, by the people for India and its adoption in January 1950 is a watershed in the history of India. The Preamble, Fundamental Rights and the Directive Principles of State Policy along with other constitutional provisions provide the basic Human Rights for the People of India.
- Human Rights enforcement calls for effective enforcement agencies. In this direction some significant acts have been passed by the Indian Parliament from time to time resulting in the formation of special commissions like the Human Rights Commissions, Special Commission for Scheduled Caste and Scheduled Tribes, National Commission for Women and the National Commission for Minorities.
- The enactment of the protection of Human Rights Act, 1993 led to the formation of the National Human Rights Commission (NHRC). The NHRC is a fully autonomous body enjoying all the powers of a civil court under the code of civil procedure. There is an enabling provision in the Protection of Human Rights Act 1993, for State Human Rights Commission to be constituted by the respective State Governments.
- UNESCO is one of the recognized specialized agency of the United Nations. It came into existence in November 4, 1946 and its competence extends to the rights relating to education, science (including social science) and culture and communications, which includes freedom of opinion and expression, and freedom of the press.
- The Montreal Protocol adopted in 1993, stresses that education for democracy is an integral aspect of education for human rights and notes that democracy is itself a human right and a prerequisite for the realization of human rights, democracy and social justice. The Protocol outlines the means by which education for human rights and democracy could be made effective and comprehensive worldwide.
- Human Rights awareness through human rights education implies awareness of rights as well as duties incumbent upon individuals, social groups and nations towards each other. This calls for building linkages and networking between individuals, institutions and agencies dealing with human rights at the global, national and grass root levels.

NOTES AND REFERENCES

1. For details see, Arjun Dev. Et.al, (ed.) (1996) *Human Rights: A Source Book*, New Delhi, NCERT. The book deals in a comprehensive manner with the provisions dealing with Human Rights in the Indian Constitution. The establishment of NHRC and enactment of various laws for the protection of human rights have also been illustrated. The chapter on human rights education with its emphasis on UNESCO and Montreal proclamations provides a fundamental insight into the subject.
2. For details see, Gokulesh Sharma, (2000), *Human Rights and Legal Remedies*, New Delhi, Deep and Deep Publications, pp. 128-147.
3. For details see, Arjun Dev et al., (ed.) n. 1.
4. *Ibid.*
5. *Ibid.*, pp. 173-186
6. *Ibid.*, pp. 182-185
7. Gokulesh Sharma, n. 2. pp. 334-341
8. *Ibid.*, pp. 379-388
9. *Ibid.*, pp. 388-391
10. As on 31 May 1996, eighty-five states were parties to the UNESCO Convention against Discrimination in Education.
11. The Recommendation concerning the Status of the Artist (1980), the Universal Copyright Convention (1952, revised in 1971) and the Recommendation of the Status of Scientific Researchers (1974).

SUGGESTED READINGS

1. Arjun Dev. Et. al, 1996, *Human Rights; A Source Book*, NCERT, New Delhi.
2. Durga Das Basu, 1994, *Human Rights in Constitutional Law*, Prentice-Hall of India, New Delhi.
3. Gokulesh Sharma, 2000, *Human Rights and Legal Remedies*, Deep & Deep Publications, New Delhi.
4. Upendra Baxi, 1987, *The Right to be Human*, Lancer International, New Delhi.
5. V.R. Krishna Iyer, 1995, *Human Rights - Judge's Miscellany*, B.R. Publishing Corporation, New Delhi.

MODEL QUESTIONS

Objective Questions (2 Marks Each)

1. Who wrote the Arthashastra?
2. What is the full form of UNESCO?

3. Mention two important functions of the SC/ST Commission?
4. When was the National Commission for Minorities constituted?

Short Questions (5 Marks Each)

1. Write a brief note on Human Rights Education.
2. Briefly discuss the powers and functions of the National Commission for Women.

Long Questions (15 Marks Each)

1. Briefly discuss the power and functions of the national Human Rights Commission.
2. Highlight the salient features of the Montreal Protocol.

5

ISSUES AND CHALLENGES

Rights of Women and Child

As early as the French Revolution, the notion that human rights included the rights of women was contested by the women revolutionaries who raised the demand for the rights of women. The women rights movement followed a separate trajectory from that of the main human rights movement as women struggled to achieve equal rights with men in the choice of work, right to education, equal pay for equal work, political rights and so on. It was only after the Second World War when women's participation in the war effort and the freedom struggles of the erstwhile colonies could not be ignored that the women's rights movement was accepted as part of the international human rights agenda. For the protection of women's rights all over the world, the UN set up in 1946, a *Commission on the Status of Women* (CSW) to monitor the situation and to promote women's rights. It adopted a *Convention on the Political Rights of Women* to legalize women's right to political participation in 1952. The U.N declared *1975 as the International Women's Year* and 1975 - 1985 as the Women's Development Decade to focus attention on the extent of discrimination against women and to promote legislative measures in member nations to end all forms of discrimination. The first *World Conference on Women* held in Mexico City in June - July 1975 adopted a *Declaration on the Equality of Women* and their contribution to the development of peace. Questions of dignity and conflict within the family were also subjects of consideration. It was endorsing the proposals of the Mexico Conference, that the UN General Assembly proclaimed the period 1976 - 85 as the *UN Decade for Women: Equality, Development and Peace.*

In 1979 the U.N adopted the *Convention for the Elimination of All Forms of Discrimination Against Women.* This document, which is in force since 1981, may be regarded as an *International Bill of Rights for Women.* The introduction to the document states, "Among the international human rights treaties, the Convention takes an important place in bringing the female half of humanity into the focus of human rights concerns. The spirit of the Convention is rooted in the goals of the United Nations: to reaffirm faith in fundamental human rights, in the dignity and worth of the human person, in the equal rights of men and women"[1]. A UN committee on the ***Elimination of Discrimination*** *(CEDAW)* was set up to monitor compliance with the convention, known as the *Women's Convention.*

The Women's Convention contains detailed provisions regarding obligations of states to undertake all appropriate measures to abolish existing laws, regulations, customs, and practices found discriminatory against women and to establish legal protection of the rights of women on an equal basis with men. It also contains provisions regarding the equal rights for women in voting and holding public offices and in education, employment and health care. It provides for equality before law and for the elimination of discrimination against women in all matters relating to marriage and family relations. However the Women's Convention does not specifically prohibit gender-based violence or place any explicit responsibilities on state parties to take action to reduce it[2]. This deficiency was left to be remedial through interpretations.

The mid- decade *1980 World Conference on Women* held in Copenhagen discussed, within the framework of equality, development and peace, problems relating to violence against women. Its conclusions held that domestic violence had serious social consequences and perpetuated itself from generation to generation, and that women must be protected from domestic violence and rape[3]. The official report of the meeting clearly mentioned the problem of violence in the home. A women's publication defined rape in a succinct manner: 'Rape is a crime of violence which uses sex as a weapon'[4].

The last of the 'Decade for Women's' Conference, the *Third World Conference on Women,* held at Nairobi in 1985, adopted *'Forward Looking Strategies for the Advancement of Women,* the *international blue print for action until the year 2000'.* The Nairobi Conference (15 - 26 July 1985) went a long way in heightening international concern over violence against women. Another conference in that year, the Seventh UN Conference on the Prevention of Crime and the Treatment of Offenders, in August - September 1985, resolved that domestic violence and rape tend to be camouflaged abuses, that they occur worldwide, that they seriously jeopardize the personal and social development of women, and are against the interests of society[5]. A UN meeting on violence in the family was held in Vienna in 1986 at the intergovernmental level. Earlier, following the Nairobi Conference, the UN General Assembly Resolution 40/36 of 29 November 1985 called for 'concerted and multi-disciplinary action', both within and outside the UN system, to deal with the problem of violence in the family. It was a very significant recognition at the international level that violence against women is an issue which affected all countries and all cultures and hence, it should be a priority for national and international action[6].

Following the Nairobi meet, the *Committee on the Elimination of Discrimination Against Women (CEDAW)* identified in 1989 five Articles relevant to violence in the Women's Convention: Art. 2 (Policy Measures to eliminate discrimination); Art 5 (Sex roles and stereotyping); Art. II (Employment rights); Art 12 (Health care and family planning); and Art. 16 (Marriage and family law).

The CWS Platform for Action prepared for the UN Fourth World Conference on Women at Beijing (4 - 15 September 1995) aimed at, among others, protecting women's human rights throughout the life cycle, and violence against women was explicitly identified as a critical area of concern. The slogan of 'women's rights are human rights' was no ordinary achievement. It lifted the world human rights movement to a new level of development[7]. The Beijing Conference adopted strong and elaborate recommendations for the protection and promotion of women's human rights. Among the strategic objectives set out, taking 'integrated measures to prevent and eliminate violence against women' was recommended with all firmness. The massive Beijing document deserves to be studied for both theory and practice of the women's movement, women's studies, and all women-related matters devoted to 'the cause of women's human rights.' Since women's rights have come to be recognized as an integral, indivisible and inalienable part of universal human rights, it ought to be the society's concern to promote and protect human rights, which are women's rights.

Despite the UDHR and the work of CSW, by and large, States have taken a rather cavalier attitude to the idea and concept of women's equality. The arguments appear to proceed like this:

(i) Sex discrimination is too trivial or not that important, or could come up for attention later on, after the larger issues of survival have been addressed;

(ii) Although regrettable, abuse of women is a cultural, private, or individual issue - it is not a political matter as such calling for state action; and

(iii) While the abuse of women is recognized, it is inevitable or so pervasive that a serious consideration is a futile exercise, as it could overwhelm other human rights questions[8].

In this connection, certain glaring realities of women's life situation should be borne in mind. It has been well said that sexism kills and being female is itself life - threatening. The following examples may be considered:

– *Before Birth*: Amniocentesis is used for sex selection leading to abortion of female fetuses and thus resulting in a disproportionate sex ratio. This phenomenon is widely prevalent in India and China.

– *During Childhood*: The World Health Organization report states that in many countries, girls are fed less, breast fed for shorter periods of time, taken to doctors less frequently, die or are physically and mentally maimed by malnutrition at higher rates than boys.

– *In Adulthood*: The denial of women's reproductive rights in the sense of control over their bodies in reproduction threatens women's lives. This is more so in conditions of poverty and poor health services.

A rapid survey of statistics shows that the extent of violence against women the world over is appalling:

- In the United States, battery is the leading cause of injury to adult women, and a rape is committed every two minutes.
- In Peru, the majority of the crimes reported to police involve women.
- In France, a very high percentage of the victims of violence are women; 5% at the hands of a spouse or lover. Similar statistics from Bangladesh, Canada, Kenya and Thailand show that more than fifty percent of female homicides are committed by family members.

- In India, eight out of ten wives are victims of violence, either domestic battery, dowry-related abuse or murder. Besides domestic violence other crimes against women in the Indian context include rape, kidnapping and abduction, molestation, sexual harassment, prostitution and Sati to name a few.

Women's Rights in the Indian Context

Against this background of a long history of global initiatives for protection and expansion of human rights in general and the rights of women in particular, it is imperative that the whole issue is examined in the Indian context.

As in the UDHR, the Preamble to the Constitution of India promises to secure for its citizens: Justice, social, economic and political; liberty of thought, expression, belief, faith and worship; and equality of status and opportunity. Further, assuring the dignity of the individuals and the unity of the country, the Constitution guarantees certain fundamental rights and freedom such as freedom of speech, protection of life and personal liberty. Thus, Indian women are the beneficiaries of Fundamental Rights in the same way as Indian men *Article 14* of the Constitution ensures "equality before law" and *Article 15* prohibits any discrimination among other grounds on that of sex. However, despite the constitutional provisions, the *Report of the Parliamentary Committee on the Status of Women* titled *Towards Equality* highlighted the fact that Indian women continued to suffer from neglect and deprivation. The report appeared as a major landmark in creating awareness about the deep-rooted disabilities faced by women in all walks of life. Moreover in conformity with the International Women's Development Decade, in India too, the decade was observed further creating awareness and mobilizing support for women's rights.

The Sixth Five-year Plan (1980 - 1985), for the first time, contained a separate chapter on Women and Development. The Plan emphasized the need for the opening up of opportunities for independent employment and income generation for women. Thereafter the objective of raising women's economic and social status has been reiterated as a policy goal. Subsequently, the *National Perspective Plan of Action for Women* was formulated outlining various administrative, legislative and other measures to promote women's development. In 1992, a *National Commission for Women* was constituted. The government has introduced a series of employment related programmes with provisions for women beneficiaries. These include *Jawahar Rozgar Yojna* with 30% reservation for women in wage employment generated; *Integrated Rural Development Programme and Training of Rural Youth for Employment* both with 40% reservation for women in self-employment generated; *Development of Women and Children in Rural Areas* fostering self employment ventures for rural women; *Support to Training and Employment Project* aimed at asset-less rural women; *Rashtriya Mahila Kosh and Mahila Samriddhi Yojana* aimed at extending credit and saving facilities for women. In extending political rights to women the 73rd and 74th Constitutional Amendment Acts (Panchayat Raj) with its 33% reservation for women is an important step. On the other hand the persistent stalling of the 84th Amendment indicates the deep-rooted bias against women's political participation in Indian society.

Some of the landmark legislations that seek to enhance and protect the economic and social status of women are as follows:

- Minimum Wages Act of 1948.
- Plantation Labour Act of 1951.
- Factories Act of 1952.
- Hindu Succession Act of 1956.
- Maternity Benefits Act of 1961.
- The Dowry Prohibition Act of 1961.
- Contract Labour (Regulation and Abolition) Act of 1966.
- Equal Remuneration Act of 1976.
- Sati Prevention Act 1987.
- The Hindu Marriage Act, 1995.

The World Congress on Human Rights met in New Delhi from 10 to 15 December 1990. The Congress recommended that national laws be examined and revised in order to remove discrimination in areas like (i) marriage (ii) inheritance (iii) matrimonial property and matrimonial relations. It has recommended the establishment of family courts based on the following principles: (a) Simplified laws and procedures (b) privacy of hearing (c) policy of appointing family court judges in equal gender proportion (d) providing counseling and mediation services as part of the court process.

The human rights for women should be considered as the collective rights of women accepted as a person with the capacity to decide or act on her own behalf. The importance of the Human Rights discourse in relation to the rights of women is that it brings in the issues of entitlements and legal provisions for implementation, so that rights are not seen as abstract concepts but as living issues.

Rights of Children

It goes without saying that todays children are tomorrows nation builders. Observance of human rights begins with the manner in which a society treats its children. A civilized and sensitive society will accord dignity to its young citizens by creating conducive conditions in which they can develop their full potential and look forward to a full and satisfying adult life[9].

The fact that children are entitled to rights have been acknowledged in various declarations and conventions from time to time. *The Geneva Declaration of the Rights of the Child, 1924* was the first convention adopted by the League of Nations to consider the rights of children[10]. *The Universal Declaration of Human Rights, 1948* confers rights to all human beings without any discrimination on the basis of age or sex. Moreover, it also stresses that a child is entitled to special care and assistance. *Article 24* of the Universal Declaration of Human Rights specifies that:

- Every child shall have without any discrimination the right to such measures of protection as are required by his status as a minor, on the part of his family, society and the state.
- Every child shall be registered immediately after birth and shall have a name.
- Every child has the right to acquire a nationality.

Article 10 of the International Convention on Economic Social and Cultural Rights specifically deal with the rights of the Child. An independent *Declaration of Rights of the Child* was passed by the *UN in 1959*. The Declaration asserts, "mankind owes to the child the best it has to give". However, it is the *Convention on the Rights of the Child, 1989*, which is regarded as landmark in the international efforts to strengthen justice, peace and freedom in the world through the protection of human rights of children. The Convention is the most complete statement of children's rights and it provides an international framework to determine the rights of the child. The Convention was adopted unanimously, by the General Assembly of UN on 20 November 1989. It entered into force on 2 September, 1990 and became international law. The Convention is the most widely ratified human rights treaty as it has been ratified, as on September 1996, by all countries except the Cook Islands, Oman, Somalia, Switzerland, the United Arab Emirates and the United States of America[11].

The Convention on the Rights of the Child, 1989, defines a child as "... a child means every human being below the age of eighteen years unless under the law applicable to the child, majority is attained earlier"[12]. The Convention's definition of childhood can be perceived as setting a basic minimum standard in view of Article 4 which declares, "nothing in the Convention or any of its provisions shall affect realization of the rights of the child, under the law of a state party". The Convention provides for the first time a clear framework and statement of rights which are worked out in greater detail than in many other human rights documents. The rights provided by the Convention can be classified into[13]:

(i) *Survival Rights* which include provisions of adequate food, shelter, clean water and primary health care.

(ii) *Development Rights* which include access to information, education, cultural activities, opportunities for rest, play and leisure and the rights to freedom of thought, conscience and religion.

(iii) *Protection Rights* include assurance of protection not only from violation of rights but also from all kinds of exploitation and cruelty. Protection is vital for especially vulnerable group among children like abandoned children, street children and displaced children.

(iv) *Participation Rights* include the right to express opinions and right to play an active role in the community and society through freedom of association.

These rights are based on the right to express views, to be heard and to participate in decision making that impacts on one's life. The child's right to be treated as a 'person' is crucial to the recognition of his/her identity and his/her capacity to exercise the rights recognized by the Convention with regard to survival, development and protection.

The Vienna Declaration on Human Rights, 1993, accelerates the dynamics of the international movement for the promotion of the rights of the child. The Vienna Declaration insists that all states should combat[14]:

- Exploitation and abuse of children by addressing their root causes.
- Devise effective measures against female infanticide, harmful child labour, sale of children, child prostitution, child pornography as well as other forms of sexual abuse.
- Organize means of improving the protection of children in armed conflicts and initiate programmes for the rehabilitation of children in war zones as well as those in especially difficult circumstances.

Despite the international efforts in the direction of protection of the rights of the child, child abuse, exploitation and victimization continues unabated. Child abuse and neglect have been defined as "the portion of harm to the child that results from human action or inaction, that is prescribed proximate and preventable"[15]. Conditions such as poverty, racism, poor health care, politically induced famine, international economic inequalities and warfare produce more suffering and death among the young than the old. The gender bias against the girl child makes her vulnerable to female infanticide, sexual abuse and discrimination in health and nutrition. Child labour too has emerged as a serious obstacle and challenge in the way of implementing the rights of the child. The term child labour may be defined as "any work by children that interferes with their full physical development and their opportunities for a desirable minimum level of education or their needed recreation" (Report of the Labour Investigation Committee, 1946).

Recognizing the significance and importance of the protection of Children's Rights, *Article 39 (I)* of the Indian Constitution states "the state shall in particular direct its policy towards seeing that children are given opportunities and facilities to develop in a healthy manner". *Article 23 of the Indian Constitution* prohibits traffic in human beings including children and *Article 24* prohibits engagement of children below the age of fourteen in hazardous jobs. Although a national policy for children was developed in 1974, Children continue to remain the most vulnerable section of the society.

Development Rights and Rights of Indigenous People

In 1986, the Declaration on the Right to Development was adopted by the General Assembly in its resolution 41/128 of 4 December. This Declaration emphasizes the importance of economic, social and cultural rights and establishes that achieving these rights is both individual and collective responsibility. The Declaration proclaims that "Development is an inalienable human right entitling everyone to contribute to and enjoy the economic, social, cultural and political development". The Declaration also states that human person as the central subject of development should be an active participant and the beneficiary of the Right to Development.

With the adoption of Vienna Declaration and Programme of Action in 1986, Right to Development got a new impetus. Moreover, the World Conferences on Human Rights reaffirmed the right to development as a universal and inalienable right and an integral part of fundamental human right.

The General Assembly by resolution 48/141 of 20 December 1993 adopted at its 48 session, established the post of High Commissioner for Human Rights. One very important function of High Commissioner was to promote and protect the realization of the right to development and enhance support from relevant bodies of the UN system for these purposes.

Although the human right to development is related to all human rights, it cannot be identified merely as the sum total of civil, cultural, economic, political and social rights. The implementation of the right to development requires first and foremost a translation of it at the domestic level. Former UN Secretary General Boutros Ghali pointed out in his *Agenda for Development* that each state had to bear the primary responsibility for its own development. The World Summit for Social Development held in 1995 at Copenhagen underlined this primary responsibility. It also emphasized that the right to development depended on over-all governance translated into coherent national policies supported by strong popular commitment. It was recognized as a means of ensuring democracy at both the national and international level as well as affecting improvement in incomes, health and social services.

The implementation of right to development depends on the fulfilment of certain conditions. These are:

i. Condition of life;

ii. Condition of work;

iii. Equality of access to resources; and

iv. Participation.

Condition of life includes basic material needs like food, shelter, health, environment and personal freedom. Condition of work includes employment, income and its equitable distribution and degree of participation in management Equality of access to resources concerns with distribution of land, financial capital, training, technology and of other productive resources. Participation includes access to information and responsiveness of decision-makers to public opinion.

The General Assembly of the UNO to implement the right to development formulated a scheme of "*Agenda for Development" in 1996.* The main objectives of the *Agenda for Development* include strengthening international co-operation for development besides enhancing the role and efficiency of the UN system in the development process. It also deals with the crucial issue of mobilization and more efficient use of resources for development. The Agenda for Development is an important blueprint for international development co-operation.

The context in which the objectives are to be pursued is spelled out in the Agenda's first chapter. The second chapter addresses the policies and measures that should be pursued and the means of implementing them. It deals with the crucial issue of the mobilization and more efficient use of resources for development both domestically and from external sources.

The third and final chapter of the agenda for development addresses the objective of enhancing the role, capacity, effectiveness and efficiency of the United Nations system. The third chapter also deals with the interaction between the United Nations and other multi- lateral development institutions, including the Bretton Woods institution and the World Trade Organization.

Developmental Rights in India

After independence, the Indian government made strategies for planned economic development. It was felt that such strategies would help break down the rigidities of the caste system and social hierarchy. The main thrusts of planning have been:

a. Introduction of income generation programmes such as Jawahar Raozgar scheme by providing finances and skills for self-employment.

b. Introducing minimum needs programmes to select poor groups to provide social consumption and social service to better their quality of life.

c. Reservation of jobs and promotion of free education. It is hoped that education will help the poor to enjoy the fruits of development.

d. Tackling low productive areas such as unfavorable soils, climate and destruction of environment which appear to be inter linked with poverty.

In India the majority of the poor are harijans, tribals, bonded labour and some other minorities. Unfortunately these groups have failed to enjoy the fruits of development. This is largely due to the lack of awareness among these deprived sections of people of their basic rights. The most essential factor contributing to this awareness is literacy — the ability to read, write and perceive, to comprehend developments beyond the community.. The irony is that while India is among the top nations in technical manpower, it also accommodates the largest numbers of illiterates with the disadvantaged communities being the worst sufferers. Even after 57 years of independence, the illiterate population of India has far exceeded the total population of the country at the time of independence. This has been the consequence of undue emphasis to higher education and the meager resources allocated to the education sector at the primary level. The allocated resources being consumed largely by universities and technical institution, the worst sufferers in this regard have been the disadvantaged communities.

Coming to land reform, 'land to the tiller' was a promise made during the independence movement. The data of land distribution and the application of land ceiling laws are not above suspicion. It is alleged that holdings have been divided and sub divided among family members of different generations to circumvent land-ceiling laws. The rural rich maintain their position through the use of muscle power and manipulation of administrative and judicial processes.

The growing disparity in the income levels in rural areas and rising aspiration among the land less and the poor has found violent expression in states like Bihar and Andhra Pradesh. Basic to all the developmental efforts is the upliftment of the scheduled caste and scheduled tribes and other sections of the marginalized population. Statutes and schemes are important, but they become meaningless in the absence of political commitment to enforce or implement them.

At the national level, states ought to take necessary measures for the realization of the right to development. It is the duty of the state to ensure equality of opportunity for all in their access to basic resources, education, health service, food, housing and employment. Popular participation in all spheres is an important factor in development. To realize this goal, the people both at the grassroots and at higher levels have to be involved in planning and implementation. The untapped human energies such as those of women need to be harnessed to achieve genuine social progress.

It must also be recognized that only an increased flow of funds into the education sector would not be sufficient to address this problem; what is equally important is the accessibility of children to schools and material resources for the effective functioning of schools. Local communities and non-governmental organizations have a major role in this regard.

At the international level the steps have to be taken individually and collectively to formulate international development policies. An effective international cooperation strategy is essential to provide help to the poor developing countries without appropriate means. The UN Resolution on Development Decade (1960) emphasized on growth based development for all the developing countries. Basically it was a call for the constant improvement in the well being of the population as a whole and of each individual[16].

The need of the hour is to initiate a process of empowering the poor to demand for their rights and realize their human rights failing which the right to development would remain merely an academic exercise.

Rights of Indigenous People

The International Labour Organization's Convention No. 107 of 1951 has defined Indigenous People as "those which having a historical continuity with pre-invasion and pre-colonial societies — consider themselves distinct from other sectors of societies now prevailing in those territories".

There are at least 300 million indigenous people in seventy states in all parts of the world. The main international instrument to protect these rights is the International Labour Organization. Convention No. 169 concerning Indigenous and Tribal People in independent countries, adopted in June 1989 which entered into force in September 1991. It affirms that no state or social group has the right to deny the identity of indigenous peoples.

Within the United Nations, the Committee on the Elimination of Racial Discrimination has considered the situation of indigenous people. A Committee on the Elimination of Racial discrimination comprising eighteen independent experts was established under Art 8 of the Convention No. 107. The Committee has several functions. Its main task is the examination of periodic reports from States Parties on the measures they have taken to implement the Convention. Governments are represented at the examination of their reports, and the Committee pursues a strategy of informal dialogue to encourage governments to comply with their obligations. In its final report, the Committee makes concluding observations on each state report, suggesting and recommending ways in which the Convention could be more effectively implemented. Some states have taken account of this by amending their constitutions and domestic laws to make racial discrimination a punishable offence, as well as establishing educational programmes and new agencies to deal with problems with racial discrimination.

The Committee has been developing measures aimed at the prevention of racial discrimination. These include early warning measures to prevent existing problems from escalating into conflicts, and confidence building initiatives towards strengthening racial tolerance and peaceful coexistence.

The Human Rights Committee also examines cases brought by indigenous persons alleging violations of their rights under Article 27 of the International Covenant on Civil and Political Rights. The *United Nations Working Group on Indigenous Population* created in 1982, is the centre of indigenous rights activities within the UN system.

It reviews government policies and makes recommendation to the sub commission on prevention of discrimination and protection of minorities. It also functions as a forum attended annually by 500 to 600 indigenous representatives who are able to exchange views in a free and democratic manner with governments, non-governmental organization and United Nations agencies.

The indigenous peoples are suffering all over the World. They are suffering from want of housing, health care, educational opportunities and employment conditions. They are also losing their land and resources, upon which their very survival depends. In many nations indigenous peoples suffer other serious human rights violation, such as arbitrary killings and disappearances. In an attempt to rectify this the

United Nation General Assembly has proclaimed the ten years starting from 10th December 1994 as the *Decade of the World's Indigenous Peoples*[17]. The goal of the Decade is to strengthen international cooperation for the solution of problems faced by indigenous peoples. The 9th August of every year is to be observed as the International Day of Indigenous People.

Rights of Indigenous People in India

The history of the indigenous people in India has been the history of their constant struggle for existence as a different cultural identity against the civilization of the colonizers. In India, at present, there are about 60 million adivasi communities. The indigenous peoples historical consciousness of their cultural identity and individuality of every community is based on the idea - *that small is beautiful.* It stands for a social value of respecting each others way of life, mutual cooperation and peaceful co-existence. The struggle of the indigenous and tribal people centre around the issues of land, forest, water, culture, transport and communication, health and hygienic, nutrition, education and identity. These demands are made to find a rightful place in the social, cultural, economic and political spheres of life in India. The thrust is also for the due recognition of the indigenous people by the government of India, which would establish their long cherished rights, and employment of their traditional habitat, and community life.

The identity of the indigenous people of India consist in their geographical, historical, linguistic and other features which give them distinct characters and distinguish them from the other peoples of the country. The indigenous people have been facing oppression and repression for a very long period of time. This calls for a strong solidarity as a part of the strategy of the liberation struggle of the indigenous people.

Land is an important ingredient of the indigenous peoples identity. But in the name of development indigenous people have been forced to evict from their own land. At times the process of sanskritization has forced them to follow Hindu process, rituals and rites and also to accept a new language. Displacement, land alienation, loss of forest and economic exploitation have marked the recent history of the indigenous people of India. In the face of centuries old oppression the indigenous people have rebelled from time to time to establish their rights. Some prominent movements of the indigenous people in India are the Narmada

Bachao Andolan, Anti-Land Alienation and Forest Protection Agitation in Telengana, Singbhum, Gujarat and Maharashtra. In the same manner, movements of ex-Tea Garden Labourers for their scheduled tribe status and industrial workers movements in Chattisgrash and Jharkhand, autonomy movements in Uttarkhand, Tripura, Andhra Pradesh and Tamil Nadu have brought into focus the plight and impoverishment of the indigenous communities in India. The Narmada valley has been a territory of protest and has become synonymous with human rights struggle in the world over. The tribals of Narmada valley have chosen to die rather live without their identity. Their struggle to control and utilize their own resources is waged on behalf of all toiling people.

It is beyond doubt that the human rights of indigenous people are being blatantly neglected and violated despite the Constitutional protection. A demand was made by the indigenous people during the UN year of Indigenous People that the tribals and semi tribals be recognized as the indigenous peoples of India. But the Government of India refused to accept this demand on the ground that adequate provision has already been made in the Constitution of India to protect their interests. In principle the Constitution of India has a number of provisions which protect the rights of the indigenous people. Article 46 of the Directive Principle of State Policy (Part - IV) of the Indian Constitution provides for the protection and promotion of the interest of the indigenous people. However in reality, demands for these very rights have been met with hostility and repression by state machinery.

Voicing the concerns of the Indigenous People, the Vienna Declaration on Human Rights instructed the governments of State Parties to protect the rights of indigenous people. The Conference also recognized the inherent dignity and the unique contribution of indigenous people to the development and plurality of society as a whole.

In India, human rights are not equally enjoyed by all. Perceptions of rights vary with socio-economic realities. Responses of people coming from different backgrounds differ. Inevitably the poor and marginalized people are compelled to toil for the basic necessities of life. Under these circumstances speaking of sustainable development and the protection of rights of marginalized people, such as the indigenous people, remains illusive. Society has so far failed to provide adequate conditions to these groups of people to enjoy their rightful entitlements. The education system has also failed to serve its purpose. Education and the sense of social responsibility do not evolve in abstraction. The motivation of the motivators is vital. There cannot be any human rights amidst acute poverty and neglect. Empowerment of this section of the people is the basic pre-requisite of any move to ensure the guarantee of their rights, which would end their politico-socio marginalization

Rights of Refugees

The 1951 UN Convention of Refugees defines a refugee as a person who owing to a "well-found fear of being persecuted for reasons of race, religion or nationality or political opinion, is outside the country of his nationality and is unable or unwilling to return because of such fears"[18]. As this definition was limited in scope, the *Organization of African Unity (OAV)* in 1969 extended the definition to include victims of aggression, occupation, foreign domination or events seriously disturbing public order. Later in 1984, the Latin American countries, in the *Cartagena Declaration of Refugees,* further extended the definition to include victims of generalized violence, international conflict and serious disturbances to public peace.

Refugee movements are involuntary movements of population. International refugee law broadly identifies a refugee as a person who:

- is outside the country of his/her nationality;
- suffers from well founded fear of persecution;and
- is unable or unwilling to return to the home country due to such fear.

Today, over thirteen million people are refugees on account of human rights violations or fear thereof. It is noteworthy that rights set out in the Refugee Convention are duplicated and complemented in the international human rights treaties and declarations, starting with the *Universal Declaration of Human Rights* and the subsequent *Covenant on Civil and Political Rights.* Some of these principles have evolved into principles of customary international law and hence are binding even on non-state parties to the treaties relating to refugees. This highlights the close relationship between human rights and refugee conventions and the fact that in effect there is no substantive difference between the two. In fact, refugee law has as its basis the *United Nations Charter* and the *Universal Declaration of Human Rights.* The 1951 Convention was drafted after the 1948 Universal Declaration and drew heavily from it. While the Universal Declaration details the basic rights of all people, Articles 13 (2) and 14 (1) specify the right to leave any country and the right to seek and enjoy asylum from persecution in other countries. These articles provide the legal framework for many refugee rights documents. On the other hand, the UN Charter provides that all member states should pledge to cooperate on pressing problems of humanitarian concern. The plight of refugees is certainly a cause for humanitarian concern. There are several other documents which have special relevance to the right of refugee because they deal with basic human rights. Among these are the *Equal Remuneration Convention, the Declaration on the Elimination of All Forms of Intolerance and of Discrimination Based on Religion or Belief, the Convention on the Political Rights of Women, the Declaration on the Rights of the Child, the Convention on the Prevention and Punishment of the Crime of Genocide and the Convention on the Non-applicability of Statutory Limitations to War Crimes and Crimes Against Humanity.*

The United Nations Convention relating to the status of Refugees of 28 July, 1951 was further clarified and extended by international instruments like the *Protocol of 1967*, the Agreement Relating to *Refugee Seamen (1957), the UN Declaration on Territorial Asylum (1967), the Convention of Stateless Person (1954)* and also through regional instruments like the *OAU Convention of 1969, the Principle Concerning the Treatment of Refugee* adopted by the Asian-African Legal Consultative Committee at its 8th Session (1966), the *Pact of San Jose (1969),* the various instruments of the Council of Europe and the *Cartagena Declaration of 1984.*

The United Nations High Commissioner for Refugees (UNHCR) was established in January 1951 by the General Assembly of the UN. The Office of the UNHCR is responsible for supervising international provisions for the protection of refugees and for seeking durable solutions by assisting governments to facilitate the voluntary repatriation of refugees and/or their integration within new national communities. The work of the *High Commissioner* is of an entirely non-political character. The UNHCR mainly deals with the following functions:

- To promote the conclusion and ratification of International Convention for the protection of refugees.
- To supervise the application of such conventions.
- To reduce the number of refugees.

- To promote the admission of refugees to the territories of state.
- To promote in signatory states the execution of measures to improve the position of refugees.
- To strive to obtain permission for refugees to transfer their assets that are essential for their resettlement.
- To obtain from the states reports concerning the number for refugees and legislative measures meant for refugees.
- To have contact with other private organizations that deal with refugees and to work for the welfare of refugees in cooperation with such private organizations.

The countries of the South Asian region are afflicted with the refugee problem. Pakistan is facing the problem of Afghan refugees; Nepal has the problem of refugees from Bhutan; Bangladesh is facing the problem of refugees from Myanmar; Sri Lanka has her own problems arising from internal displacement and India has the problem of Chakma refugees from Bangladesh, Tamil refugees from Sri Lanka, Tibetan refugees, Bhutanese refugees, Arakanese refugees from Myanmar and refugees from some other countries. India also has the problem of internally displaced Kashmiri Pandits. Refugees in South Asia constitute approximately 12 percent of the global refugee population. Large numbers of refugees in the region are produced by South Asian countries and also absorbed and hosted by countries within the region. This has resulted in some valuable experiences in refugee management by South Asian countries that may mainly be attributed to various reasons peculiar to this region such as:

- Ease of physical accessibility;
- Cultural and linguistic affinity; and
- Political support of host governments.

Three broad refugee generating factors in South Asia may be identified. *First,* the breakdown of colonial rule and the rationalization of some of the colonial policies pre-eminently the policy of divide and rule which led to massive cross-border flows. *Second* state and nation-building processes which precipitated political, ethnic and religious conflicts and also adversely affected economic and environmental conditions thus forcing people to migrate within and outside their countries. *The third factor* cited is extra-regional developments leading to the entry of refugees from outside the region[19].

The fact is that every country in the region is multi-ethnic, multi-religious and multi-cultural with the possible exception of Maldives and increasingly Bhutan. This provides a fertile ground for centrifugal tendencies. To this should be added the historical background - the concepts of nationalism, democracy and secularism are not inherent to the region but are borrowed from the West, a legacy, in fact, of colonialism. With time each state has begun to modify these concepts to suit its own needs. With the narrowing down of these concepts certain groups whether ethnic, religious or otherwise have begun to find themselves marginalized. The result is alienation, the growth of subnationalism and insurgency. Millions of South Asians have therefore crossed borders and sought refuge in other countries within the region and at times even outside the region.

In regard to *Refugee Rights* in India, although India has not signed the UN Convention of 1951 relating to the status of refugees, she has acceded to the two *1966 Covenants on Civil and Political Rights and Economic, Social and Cultural Rights.* However, these have not been integrated into the municipal laws of the country and are thus not enforceable in courts of law. This does not mean that India can overlook or ignore refugee rights. The Indian Constitution guarantees fundamental rights, some of which are equally available to all persons whether citizens or aliens. Subject to these rights, Parliament has the exclusive power to make laws with respect to aliens and related matters. Furthermore, *Article 51* of the Indian Constitution encourages the State to endeavour to promote peace and security and foster respect for international law and treaty obligations as well. *Article 21* of the Constitution also states that "no person shall be deprived of life or personal liberty except accordance to procedure established by law". This is applicable to refugees as well.

It is to be noted and appreciated that the position of a refugee is to be distinguished from that of other aliens. The traumatic conditions of flight from country of origin, accompanying hardships, vulnerability and insecurity require specific treatment which is organized and structured, and hence specific legislation relating to the treatment and welfare of refugees is necessary. In pursuance to the protection of basic human rights of refugees seeking asylum in India, national legislation is essential for ensuring the establishment of a regulated process of refugee status determination, reception and assistance, which would guarantee fair treatment to asylum seekers.

Human Rights and the Challenge of Ethnic Conflicts and Political and Social Violence

A stark reality of civil society today is that it is characterized by an increasing level of socio-political violence. Increasingly, ethnic groups and social classes are negotiating with the state in the idiom of violence as a means of articulating their demands. The rise of this phenomenon is largely an outcome of socio-political and economic processes. In a situation of scarce resources, the state becomes the principal means of access to and control of resources. This results in a scenario where the state and its resources become objects of considerable political attention. When the politicized social group fail to maneuver, negotiate and bargain within the political space, they resort to violence. The politics of identity formation and assertion are enmeshed in secular economic interests. Violence has emerged as a complex issue of political inquiry. Analysts invariably take recourse to socio-psychological, cultural and anthropological explanations to understand this phenomenon[20].

As opposed to other forms of violence, socio-political violence is a group phenomenon carried out with the intent of having an impact on the political system. It is the use of force for the resolution of conflicts in society that mainly originate from socio-political, economic, ethnic and cultural causes and that find expression in various forms of collective action. Political violence need not always be overt physical armed violence. Violence may be in-built into the structure - characterized as structural violence - violence that is implicit in the structure domination and inequality in a society. This type of violence is exerted by situations, institutions, social, political and economic structures, which are legitimized by the prevailing juridical order and socio-political, and economic institutions[21].

Political violence emerges within a certain socio-political and economic context. It is generally designated for a reordering purpose which may be to realize justice and equity, to achieve territorial autonomy or to impose one's religious and doctrinal beliefs. In democratic societies, political violence suggests institutional weaknesses. In the context of the Third World countries, political violence is largely an outcome of the nation-state building process. The developing societies are fragmented with too many ethnic religious and linguistic differences. Most of these developing states are of a multiethnic character, consisting of several nations. Hence, ethnicity as a category of conflict exists not only at the level of consciousness, but it is also a reflection in consciousness of very real, concrete and material circumstances.

Ethnicity has been variously expressed as assertion of cultures, communal upsurges, revivalism of religions, voices of marginalized peoples, regions and nationalities. It represents the affirmation of diversity, of indigenous authenticity, of organic as against televised or classicized cultures. At the present juncture of world history ethnicity takes on both dominating and liberating forms. Its more human version includes other identities and thus respects plurality. Its more defiant version excludes other identities. What is more, the two versions are found to be caught in a strange partnership against the more secular drives of the modern state. In the overall context of the project of modernity, ethnicity has emerged as a strategy of purposive mobilization in a civic society. It has been argued that ethnicity represents a revolt against the excesses of the modern project of shaping the whole of humanity around the three pivots of modernity — the state system and a 'world culture' based on modern technology, a pervasive communications and information order and a 'universalizing education system'[22]. The project of modernity entails a new mode of homogenizing and straitjacketing the whole world and ethnicity is thus both a response and reaction to the modern conception of universalization. It has threefold claim. *First,* it is the effort to project a particular into a universal, expecting the rest of the world to accept the worldview and organizing principles of that particular. *Second,* it is the effort to universalize secular and temporal space. *Third,* the modernist perspective on universalization takes upon itself the task of fragmenting and splintering all other social and ethical cohesions and imposing its globalizing will and power on all others[23].

The upsurge of negative identities has speedily eroded not just state authority but has also resulted in social breakdown. It has also legitimized a new brand of politics that combines communal crimes, fundamentalist slogans and pure terrorism. This has resulted in the destruction and decay of institutions; of erosion of legitimate authority; of the decline of civil society; and of the collapse of the democratic state that had given cohesion to civil society without undermining its pluralistic character. It is the growing convergence between a secular and technocratic vision of the state and the search for a chauvinist ideology that provides the new setting for a more exclusive and negative thrust of ethnicity. Such a thrust is drawing its inspiration from new and unsuspected sources; from the state which is supposed to be secular; from the modernist national elite which is supposed to provide correctives to parochial tendencies; from the security establishment which is supposed to be committed to democratic values; from science and technology elite which is supposed to breathe 'scientific temper'; from the votaries of 'high culture' who are supposed to be the custodians of humanism, compassion and catholicity[24].

Some analysts have tried to explain the cause of political violence as product of unresponsive governments. However, in reality political violence is attendant even in those states, which are not repressive or unresponsive. This makes it imperative to seek explanations in the socio-political and material bases of society. Samuel P. Huntington has given primacy to political and institutional factors and emphasized disequilibrium within the political sector as the primary cause of violence. According to him if a country's institutional procedures for political participation are inadequate in comparison to the people's expectations for participation, this could lead to unrest and anti regime activity. As a result of mobilization, new social forces enter the political arena, but the political structure does not provide channels for their participation in politics, thereby leading to civil strife[25].

Government policies almost always have significant effects on the course and trajectory of socio-political violence in the country in question, Misguided or malicious policies can aggravate problems and turn potentially violent situations into deadly confrontations. In Sri Lanka, for example, decades of discriminatory government policies with respect to citizenship, language, religion, education and government employment, alienated and radicalized the country's Tamil minority, and ultimately led to open rebellion and civil war. In Pakistan, the government's favoured treatment of Punjabis in West Pakistan precipitated East Pakistan's secession in 1971. The Burmese government's assimilationist agenda, its refusal to grant real autonomy to minorities in out laying regions, its anti-democratic impulses, and its heavy reliance on military force are the main reasons why Burma has experienced political violence throughout most of its post-colonial history.

In other cases, comparatively benign policies have helped to hold countries together under extraordinarily difficult circumstances. Perhaps the best example of this in Asia is India, a country with a large population and tremendous diversity. Although the policies of the Indian government have not always been well conceived, well executed or non-violent in nature, the country's .democratic traditions and the government's comparatively temperate policies with respect to religious issues, language issues, education and regional autonomy have undeniably, played key roles in dampening tensions and keeping a potentially fragile country from disintegrating.

When thinking about how government policies influence ethnic relations, three sets of distinctions should be kept in mind. *First*, governments influence ethnic relations through both general policies aimed at the country as a whole and specific policy targeted at specific ethnic issues. The former includes basic decisions about political structures as well as decisions about broad economic policies. The latter include citizenship policies, civil rights and minority rights policies, policies on religion and religious groups, language policies, education policies, and economic policies aimed at improving the lot of one group or another. *Second*, governments influence ethnic relations both by design and by accident. In some cases, governments make deliberate, well-intentioned efforts to address ethnic problems, improve the position of ethnic minorities and promote better ethnic relations. In all too many cases however, leaders and governments make deliberate efforts to promote the interests of some ethnic groups over others and to discriminate politically and economically against ethnic minorities. This often grows out of a political need to take care of ethnic constituencies, which can be key to getting in or staying in power. *Third*, governments influence ethnic relations through inaction[26].

The starting point for analyzing government policies has to be a consideration of policy settings. Policies are not formulated or implemented in vacuums. Different governments have to contend with different kinds of problems and challenges and these problems change over time, both in response to whatever governments do and do not do, and in response to other domestic, regional and international developments. Against this situational background, four broad parameters frame government policies: *Policy goals*, *Policy instruments, Policy patterns* and *Generic policy problems*. It is imperative that governments try and dampen tensions by trying to depoliticize them. In practical terms, this means establishing and maintaining rule of law; favouring civic over ethnic conceptions of nationalism and citizenship, favouring broad civil rights protections over specific minority rights initiatives;

supporting secularism over the establishment of official state religion; respecting linguistic diversity and promoting multi-lingualism; and building broad based consensus for preferential and affirmative action policies in the educational and economic arenas. The track record of democracies in dealing with ethnic problems in quite good in important respects. Democracies provide mechanisms for groups, large and small to participate in the formation of governments, be represented in decision-making circles, and to have influence over policy. Democracies also provide mechanisms for people to express their displeasure with policies and to chart new, more constructive policy courses.

The positive promise however lies in the building of a social order, which celebrates diversity and organic unity, and is organized around principles of equity, justice, peace and dignity. It is only through a clear and coherent identification with new social consciousness being thrown up by social movements like the human rights movement, the survival movements, the ecology movements and peace movements, that the lost spaces in civil society can be reclaimed.

Global Terrorism and Human Rights

Global Terrorism today has emerged as one of the most serious challenge to human rights. It is one of the most ruthless and destructive instrument of any international, internal, ethnic or religious conflicts in contemporary times. As a form of organized violence, it has infected almost all continents - Europe, the Americas, Asia and Africa. As a method of conducting warfare, terrorism cuts through sovereign boundaries with utmost freedom. More often than not, it carries no distinct national banner as its executors and combatants are of mixed nationality. The only source of cohesion among the members is their common faith in the use of organized and systematic violence to achieve political, religious, cultist or personal objective.

Almost all the states have had a taste of terrorism in one way or another in recent times. Afghanistan, Brazil, Myanmar, Canada, Colombia, Egypt, Indonesia, Israel, Italy, Japan, Jordan, Lebanon, Pakistan, the Philippines, EL Salvador, Spain, Sri Lanka, Thailand, Turkey, the United Kingdom, the United States, Uruguay and many others. Currently some 1500 terrorist groups, parties or organizations are operating worldwide. Some important terrorist groups operating in these countries have been identified as: Harkatul Ansar, Hizbullah, Italian Red Brigade, Japanese Red Army, Kashmir Liberation Tigers, Kurdistan Workers Party, Fatah

Revolutionary Command, Liberation Tigers of Tamil Eelam, Laskar-e-Taiba, Al-Qaida, Nationalist Socialist Council of Nagalim, People's War Group, Palestine Liberation Front, Tupac Amoro Revolutionary Movement, Revolutionary Armed Forces of Columbia, National Liberation Front of Tripura, Hamas, Al-Jihad and so on.

Although the concept of "Terrorism" has been in public discourse for more than two hundred years, a truly comprehensive and universally accepted definition of the term is yet to emerge Scholarly attempt in this regards have produced little result[27]. Defining the concept has proved to be difficult task because of various reasons. The *first* and foremost relates to the element of ***subjectivity.*** Often the concept is influenced by subjective factors such as one's own view of justice, freedom, national rights, human rights and strategic interest. Further, more often than not the issue of terrorism is treated on the basis of ethics and morality, and not merely legality. As a result, terrorism as a political instrument has become a deeply divided and emotive issue in recent years. There is hardly any act of terrorist violence which has evoked a uniform response. In this sense, one man's "terrorist" is another man's "freedom fighter"[28]. Much depends on which side of the divide one is viewing the phenomenon from.

A second definitional problem is that there is no terrorism per se; there are different kinds of terrorisms[29]. Different actors use terrorism for different objectives. The variety of actors include individuals, nation-state and non-state actors such as liberation movements, revolutionary organizations, secessionist outfits, underground movements and religious movements.

Terrorism is difficult to define for yet another reason; its character keeps changing from time to time. This refers to its methods, lethality, targets, aims, area of operation and the character of people who resort to terrorism.

It goes without saying, that as there is no agreed definition of terrorism internationally it has not been possible to have an international convention on terrorism. However, what is clear it that all forms of violence is not terrorism. Terrorism as a political instrument has been used by a variety of actors and for a variety of purposes over the years. Therefore, the construction of a foolproof, all inclusive typology is not only not possible but would also amount to an oversimplification of a highly complex and fast changing phenomenon. However, on the basis of motivations and actors one can outline a broad and flexible typology which would include the following: *terrorism by non-state actors, terrorism by state actors,* and terrorism guided by religious motivations or the so called "*post-modern terrorism*".

Terrorism by non-state actors refers to terrorist activities by revolutionary movements, national liberation movements and separatist organizations. Terms like revolutionary terrorism, nationalist terrorism and separatist terrorism are also used in this context depending on the nature, ideology and objectives of organizations. Subjects in various parts of Asia and Africa clamored for independence and self-determination and waged valiant struggles against their European colonial masters. Most of these nationalist and anti-colonist movements adopted an ideology that represented a combination of nationalist and Marxist-Leninist ideas. Contemporary examples of organizations whose political programmes reflected such a combination include the *Irish Revolutionary Army, the Basque, Freedom de Liberation Quebec* and several Palestinian organizations within the *Palestine Liberation Organization.*

Terrorism by state actors can be of two types: *state terrorism and state-sponsored terrorism*. The first one refers to a situation where a particular state itself is involved in initiating, planning and executing terrorist acts to deal with internal dissent, extremist violence and separatist terrorism. It is normally carried out by the coercive apparatus of the state concerned and its act are generally legitimized as 'counter-terrorist' operations[30]. More often than not these operations form of the state's national security agenda. In the second type, the concerned state does not get directly involved in terrorist operations against its adversary; the terror campaign is waged through proxies. This can be done through providing infrastructural support, technological back up, weapons supply, training facilities and financial assistance, to the opponents of the adversary. The concerned state can also, at times make use of its own intelligence agencies. The area of operation may not remain confined to the geographical limits of the adversary and the targets may include both high-profile individuals and strategic interests and institutions. Generally a state which is unwilling or unable to take on its adversary through established international norms resorts to such type of terrorist activities.

In the 1990s many incidents of 'spectacular terrorist violence' shocked the international community. These included the 1993 World Trade Centre Bombings in New York; 1995 Aum Shinrikyo's attack of the Tokyo subway through Sarin gas; the 1995 Oklahoma city bombings, and the 1998 simultaneous bombing of U.S. embassies in Nairobi, Kenya and Dar-es-Salaam, Tanzania. The most recent and shocking terrorist attack has been the September 11, 2001 strike in New York, Washington and Pennsylvania.

Scholars interpreted these as the 'unmistakable harbingers' of a *New Terrorism*, the so-called postmodern terrorism[31]. The predominant motivation behind this new terrorism is religious zeal coupled with messianic fervour; most of the earlier groups which took resort to terrorism in varying degrees had secular nationalist or separatist goals and beliefs, many deriving their inspiration from or guided by the ideas of Marx and Lenin. By contrast it has been found that the proportion of terrorist groups motivated mostly by religious consideration has increased significantly in recent times. Further, a linkage has also been noticed between religious motivations and the increasing lethality of attacks[32]. In most cases these groups seek to provide religious sanctity and legitimacy by putting 'political issues and struggles within a sacred context.'

Apart from religious motivations, the new terrorism also differs from the old type in many other aspects: organizational structure, recruitment base, external support (state sponsors), resource base, technological superiority, operational reach, scale of violence and lethality of attack. The perpetrators of new terrorism are not organized hierarchically in well-defined command and control structure like their earlier counterparts. The recruitment base is very wide and flexible; many volunteers come with technical skills with formal education in computer science or engineering with proper established positions in society that provide them the logistic base of modern communication technology[33]. The 'New Terrorism' debate has brought to the centre stage issues of critical concern. There is little dispute over the fact that the nature of terrorism and the attitude of the individuals who use this as an instrument of their struggle have undergone a change. The revolutionary progress in the field of information and communication technology has given a new dimension to the phenomenon of terrorism. The increasing tendency to use religion as a cover needs to be seen in the wider context of the end of the Cold War, the changed equations in the international power structure and the upsurge of ethno-religious and intrastate conflicts.

The following are some broad generalizations of what constitutes terrorism:

- It symbolizes premeditated violent activity to attain political objectives.
- The acts of violence committed by the terrorists are seen by the society in which they take place as unconventional.
- The direct objective is not the physical suppression of the enemy's conventional forces but to put psychological pressure on the enemy.
- It is directed towards a wider audience than the actual victims of violence.
- External support is crucial for the survival and success of the group. Invariably, it enjoys outside links in terms of ideology, finance, military technology and religion.
- New weapons and technological advances have greatly facilitated the frequency and intensity of terrorist operations.
- Operations are not confined to the territorial limits of enemy or adversary.
- It is against the established international norms of conflict and conflict resolution.

The causes of terrorism are country specific and there is no cause of terrorism that can be applied uniformly to all the countries of the world. However some critical variables can be identified:

- Persistence of extreme poverty and accompanying deprivations such as unemployment, low levels of literacy and limited access to health services.
- Years of misgovernance which has made violence the only means of bringing about a change.
- Brutal suppression of human rights over an extended period of time.
- Alienation of whole cultural or ethnic groups brought about by threats to life by frequent communal violence, destruction of means of livelihood, historical humiliation, and continuing *de facto* discriminations in jobs and opportunities.
- Narrowing of mind brought about by fundamentalist indoctrination.

- Social and political injustice.
- Loss of cultural identities due to the homogenization process associated with globalization.
- Use of non-state actors by external powers in pursuit of their political or strategic goals.

The international community is experiencing the specter of terrorism and is aware of its fallout on socio-economic and political life. Security is key to the existence and progress of a nation. Terrorism strikes at the very foundation of civilized existence. In case of India, terrorism has had the following fallout:

- It has made violence a daily occurrence.
- It has de-sensitized civil society.
- It has led to the deterioration of law and order.
- It has led to flight of capital.
- It has led to the subversion of democratic and constitutional process.
- It has emerged as a serious threat to the secular fabric of the country.
- It has raised the political, military and financial costs of governance.
- It has led to the violation of human rights by both the terrorists and security forces.

Despite the serious challenge posed by terrorism to the well being of nation states, a common agreed formula to cope with this threat is yet to emerge. Every nation has its own interpretation and methodology to deal with this challenge. A problem of this magnitude cannot be countered until and unless sincere efforts are made at the national, regional and international levels for developing a cooperative framework.

International law does not possess requisite instrument to face terrorism effectively. At the international level variety of measures and counter measures have been designed for checking the menace of terrorism. Some important International Conventions on Terrorism are: The Convention on Offences and Certain other Acts Committed on Board Aircrafts (Tokyo, 1983), the Convention for the Suppression of Unlawful Acts against the Safety of Civil Aviation (Montreal, 1971), the

Convention on the Prevention and Punishment of Crimes against Internationally Protected Persons, including Diplomatic Agents (New York, 1973), the Convention on the Physical Protection of Nuclear Material (Vienna 1980). The UN General Assembly adopted the Convention Against the Taking of Hostages in 1979 and the Convention on the Safety of United Nations and Associates Personnel in 1994 and the International Convention for the Suppression of Terrorists Bombing in 1997.

Global terrorism though universally condemned cannot be eliminated by a policy of counter measure or by acts of adopting Conventions. It calls for collaborative efforts at the global level. Human rights group can certainly play an important role in educating the masses about the futility of the terrorist activities. A dispassionate understanding of the phenomenon can help devise coping strategies.

ENVIRONMENTAL ISSUES AND HUMAN RIGHTS

The agenda set recently for a review of global politics and future of human well -being has brought the environmental components of security into the Human Rights discourse. Thus, the concept 'environmental security' arose at a time when there was already an intellectual ferment in the field of international security in the Western World. The need for reconceptualizing the traditional understanding of security due to the latter's utter inadequacy was felt. The need was to secure the people living within the state. Environmental degradation has been perceived as an equal if not greater threat to humanity than a military threat.

Environmental security as a concept encompassing non-military aspects was officially mentioned for the first time in the *International Conference on the Relationship between Disarmament and Development*, convened by the United Nations General Assembly in New York from 24 August to 11 September 1987. The final document adopted by consensus by the representatives from 150 participating states says:

> Recently non-military threats to security have moved to the forefront of global concern. Underdevelopment and the declining prospect for development as well as mismanagement and waste of resources constitute challenges to security. The degradation of the environment presents a threat to sustainable development... Mass poverty,

illiteracy, disease, squalor and malnutrition affecting a large proportion of the World's population often become the cause of social strain, tension and strife[34].

Going further than this, the report by the *World Commission on Environment and Development* (Brundtland Report) entitled 'Our Common Future' stressed the influence of environmental degradation on the relationship between states. It attempted to establish the conflictual relationship between states as:

> Environmental stress is both a cause and effect of political tension and military conflict. Nations have often fought to assert to resist control over raw materials, energy supplies, land, river basin, sea passages and other key environmental resources. Such conflicts are likely to increase as these resources become scarcer and competition for them will increase[35].

There is a clear-cut connection between environment and human well being. Two distinct features of environmental security are: *First,* the environmental causes of conflict; *Second,* the impact of environmental degradation on overall economy, health and life of the people. Environmental degradation in terms of greenhouse gases, carbon dioxide emission, thinning of ozone layer, land degradation, water scarcity, deforestation, desertification and other calamities like flood and cyclone caused by anthropogenic and natural reasons have been a threat to the well being of people.

To clarify the key issues in the environmental debate, there is need to introduce two dimensions: *intentionality and time* perspective of threats. As observed, social facts are products of collective intentionality which, in this context refers to the role and impact of human agents in changing the environment and producing through it political outcomes. *Intentional* environmental threats to security include ecological vandalism and the deliberate destruction of the environment for political and military purpose that lead to the weakening of the target society and the loss of human life. *Unintentional* environmental threats refer to both large scale ecological changes and byproducts of commercial activities such as pollution and the depletion of resources, which have seldom been their primary objectives[36].

In the *temporal perspective*, environmental changes can have either immediate or long-term effects on national and human security. *Immediate* effects are produced, for example, by floods, earthquakes, and droughts which affect the population of the target society without much delay. Other environment changes affect security only over a *long term* as their effects accumulate over decades or even centuries and responsibility can seldom be attributed to any single actor or generation.

Types of Environmental Threats

The main categories of environmental security threats are *contextual, contaminating* and *competitive. Contextual* environmental threats have a long gestation period and therefore the probability of their acute occurrence is low. When the risks finally materialize their physical and social consequences can be massive. *Contaminating* threats are likely results of modern industrial and military activities, which involve dumping pollutants in rivers and seas or sowing nitrogen or sulphuric acids in the air. These threats often cross national boundaries and thus adversely affect the welfare of people in a given region or sea basin. Finally, environmental threats can result from *competition* for natural resources by governments and transnational corporations. Such rivalries are motivated by material interests in gaining control of, or access to limited renewable or non-renewable resources and are, therefore, intentional.

There are different kinds of environmental conflicts and they can be classified by their *cause*, *domain and intensity*. In terms of *causes*, conflicts are fostered either by material, structural, institutional or identity causes. *Material conflicts* are about the distribution of scarce renewal or nonrenewable resources among the actors. *Structural conflicts* boil down to the struggle for positions, interests, and reputation in social and political hierarchies. *Institutional conflicts* focus on the exercise of political power in society: who in entitled to wield power and through what institutions; when is power legitimate; and does established power face a challenge from the opposition? Finally, *identity conflicts* concern the definition by both individual and collective actors of the self in relation to the other.

The *domain* of conflict can be *global, regional, national or local. Global conflicts* affect the entire planet through their impact on its ecosystem, people, or the global political and economic system. *Regional conflicts* concern only a given geographical subsystem which may comprise either a certain coherent group of states or an integrated set of transnational relations across borders. *National conflicts* are, as a rule, defined by the state - society relationship in which actors are competing for material and political power, or the legitimacy of its exercise.

Local conflicts have the most limited domain as they affect only a specific community with in a society.

Thomas Horner-Dixon has specified three different types of conflicts and spelt out their environmental implications. *Simple scarcity conflicts* are about a zero-sum division of resources, usually water, fish or agricultural land. *Group-identity conflicts* are due to cultural strife brought about by environmentally induced mass movements of people. *Relative-deprivation conflicts* result from meagre economic performance due to environmental problems, which, in turn, elicit political discontent from the impoverished people. Conflicts fostered by inter - group hostilities and relative deprivation are both primarily local or national in their scope, although they may well have international, repercussions. Scarcity conflicts are more likely to have inter- state and even regional dimension[37].

It is likely that interstate conflicts over the *allocation of environmental and economic burdens* will intensify in the future and will increasingly shape the political agenda and thus the dynamics of international relations. This latent and sometimes manifest, conflict will pit leading industrial powers in North America and Western Europe against emerging power centres of the South, in particular Brazil, China, India, Indonesia and to a lesser degree Russia.

Environmental Rights

Environment protection has emerged as an international concern. The severity of environmental degradation has become a major threat to human life. On account of multidimensional effect of this phenomenon the right to healthy environment has come to be universally accepted as a human right.

Every human being is entitled to live in a healthy environment. Clean air and water are essential for basic human existence. The United Nations Conference on the Environment held at Stockholm in June 1972 proclaimed the right of human beings to a healthy environment. It also adopted an action plan to be undertaken by governments and international organizations. The historic Stockholm Conference of 1972 represents the first major global effort to address the issue of the protection and improvement of the environment. The Conference emphasized that the natural resources of the earth including the air, water, land, flora and fauna should be safeguarded and preserved for the benefit of present and future generations. It established a balance between the sovereign right of states to use one's own natural resources and the duty to avoid damage to others.

Not all the global environmental problems were foreseen in 1972. There is a deepening environmental crisis in all the parts of the world. Some important concerns relate to the depletion of the ozone layer, global warning, deforestation and the poisoning of the air, water and soil. Many of there problems are global in scope and can be tackled only at the global level. The London Dumping Convention of 1975 is one such important convention, which prohibits the dumping by ships of hazardous industrial wastes into the sea. The United Nations Convention on the Law of the Sea of 1982 is also another important Convention, which specifically concerns with the protection of the maritime environment.

The Food and Agricultural Organization of the UNO (FAO) has been very active in the area of food safety and pesticide. FAO's international code on the distribution of the use of pesticides, adopted in 1985, is designed to promote the safe and efficient use of particles and to prevent their misuse.

The concept of the right to safe and clean environment has emerged as a basic human right. Some countries have introduced environmental protection in their constitutions. For example, Article 24 of the Greek Constitution says, "Protection of the natural and cultural environment is a duty of the state. The state is directed to adopt special prohibitive measures for the preservation of the environment". A number of other States like Sri Lanka, China, Switzerland and some European countries have similar guidelines in their constitutions. The Constitutions of a few US states have also incorporated the right to clean and safe environment.

India has taken a lead in giving a constitutional status to environment protection. Part IV of the Indian Constitution states that the State shall endeavour to protect and improve the environment by safeguarding the forests and wild life of the country. Article 51 A of the Fundamental Duties prescribes "it shall be the duty of every citizen of India to protect and improve the natural environment including forests, lakes, rivers and wild life and to have compassion for living creatures". Water (Prevention and Control of Pollution) Act 1974, and Environment Protection Act 1986 indicate the measures taken by the government to safeguard the environment. Apart from constitutional safeguards there is a contingent of about more than three hundred central and state legislations which have a direct or an indirect bearing on the environment.

In India there are large number of legislation to protect the environment. Some of these are: Acts on ... Explosive Substances, Preservation of Forest, Wild Life, Inflammable Substances etc. Despite these laws environmental degradation has become an acute problem in India. This is on account of the following reasons:

- Many of the laws are outdated.
- They lack statements of explicit policy objectives.
- They are mutually inconsistent.
- They lack adequate provisions for helping the implementing machinery.
- There is no procedure for reviewing the laws.

To improve the situation, there is need for new legislation in the areas of action not covered by the present laws and the introduction of environment protection in the concurrent list of the seventh schedule. Such legal measures are to be codified as basic human rights.

POINTS TO REMEMBER

- Women's Rights are integral to human rights. The importance of the human rights discourse in relation to the rights of women is that it brings in the issues of entitlements and legal provisions for implementation, so that rights are not seen as abstract concepts but as living issues. The human rights for women should be considered as the collective rights of women accepted as a person with the capacity to decade or act on her behalf.
- Children are entitled to rights as much as any other section of the society. A civilized and sensitive society will accord dignity to its young citizens by creating conducive conditions in which they can develop their full potential and look forward to a full and satisfying adult life.
- Developmental Rights are central to human rights discourse. They are indivisible and interdependent. Right to Development is based on the premise that all individuals are entitled to enjoy economic, social, cultural and political development in the absence of which human rights and fundamental freedoms cannot be realized. Human

beings ought to be the active participant and beneficiary of the right to development. The Rights of Indigenous People have to be understood in the context of Development Rights. The struggles of the indigenous people all over the world is centered around the issues of economic survival and recognition of identity.

- Refugee movements are involuntary movements of population. Today, over thirteen million people are refugees on account of human rights violations or fear thereof. Refugees is South Asia constitute approximately 12 percent of the global population. Besides the 1951 UN Convention for Refugees there are many international and regional documents that lay down rights for refugees.
- Civil society today is characterized by an increasing level of ethnic conflicts and socio-political violence. The rise of this phenomenon is largely an outcome of socio-political and economic process. When politicized social groups fail to manoeuver, negotiate and bargain within the political space, they resort to violence the fallout of which has a direct bearing on human welfare and human rights. Government policies almost always have significant effects on the course and trajectory of socio-political violence.
- In contemporary times, global terrorism has emerged as one of the most ruthless and destructive instrument of any international, internal, ethnic or religious conflicts. As a form of organized violence, it has infected almost all continents - Europe, the Americas, Asia and Africa - and has emerged as a serious challenge to the international human rights regime. Combating a problem of this magnitude calls for the development of a cooperative framework at the national, regional and international levels.
- Environmental issues have become a significant factor in international politics. There is now wide awareness of the environmental degradation that can attend human activity and the threats these can pose to human welfare. The causes of environmental degradation are fundamentally economic and demographic, the remedies often have to do with industrial adoption, internal regulation or international co-operation touching on matters far removed from questions of force and conflict. Nevertheless, environmental problems can be a source of political conflict between states and can contribute to violence within and between states and thus lead to human rights violation.

NOTES AND REFERENCES

1. For details see Joan Fitzpatrick, 'The Use of International Human Rights Norms to Combat Violence Against Women', in Rebecca J. Cook (ed.), *Human Rights of Women: National and International Perspectives*, Philadelphia, University of Pennsylvania Press, 1995.
2. *Ibid.*, P. 532.
3. *Ibid.*, p. 536.
4. *Women's Realities, Women's Choices: An Introduction to Women's Studies Collective*, New York, Oxford University Press, 1983, p. 467.
5. *In Human Rights of Women* n.1, p. 536.
6. Margaret Schuler, (ed.) *Freedom From Violence: Women's Strategies From Around The World*, New York, Women, Law and Development OEF International, 1992, p. 4.
7. For details see D.P. Barooah's paper entitled 'Reflections On Defining Women's Rights As Human Rights', *International Round Table, Research Committee 7 of International Political Science Association*, Chandigarh, Punjab University, 17 - 21 August, 1993.
8. *Ibid.*
9. *Human Rights: The Rights of the Child*, Fact Sheet No. 10, United Nations.
10. Sunil Deshta and Kiran Deshta, *Law and Menace of Child Labour*, New Delhi, Anmol Publications, 2000, p. 3.
11. S.K. Khanna, *Children and the Human Rights*, New Delhi, Commonwealth Publishers, 1998, pp. 25-26
12. Article 1, *Convention on the Rights of the Child*
13. Savitri Goonesekere, *Children, Law and Justice*, New Delhi, Sage Publications, 1998, p. 85.
14. Upendra Baxi, 'Reclaiming Our Common Future: Human Rights of Children', in the *Child and the Law*, UNICEF, New Delhi, India Country Office, 1994, p. 12.
15. B.K. Raina, 'Child and Human rights: an Insight' in B.P. Singh Sehgal (ed.) *Human Rights in India*, New Delhi, Deep and Deep Publications, 1994, p. 184.
16. For details see M.R. Redclift, *Sustainable Development: Exploring the Contradictions*, London, Metheum Publications, 1987.
17. Resolution 48/163 of 21 December 1993.
18. Office of the UN High Commissioner of Refugees, *Collection of International Instruments Concerning Refugees*, Geneva, 1990, p. 11.
19. S.D. Muni and Lok Raj Baral, *Refugee and Regional Security in South Asia*, New Delhi, 1996.
20. For details see Veena Das, "Time, Self and Community: Features of the Sikh Militant Discourse" in Veena Das, *Critical Events: An anthropological Perspective on Contemporary India*, Delhi, Oxford University Press, 1995, pp. 118-36.

21. John Galtung, *Peace by Peaceful Means: Peace and Conflict, Development and Civilization,* London, Sage Publications, 1996, p. 157.
22. See Rajani Kothari, "Ethnicity" in Kumar David and S. Kadirgamar (eds.) *Ethnicity, Identity and Crisis,* Hongkong, Arena Press, 1996, p. 16.
23. *Ibid.*
24. *Ibid.*, p. 31.
25. For details see Samuel P. Huntington, *Political Order in Changing Societies,* New Haven, Yale University Press, 1968, pp. 274 - 75.
26. For details see Michael E. Brown, "The Impact of Government Policies on Ethnic Relations" in Michael E. Brown and Sumit Ganguly (eds.), *Government Policies and Ethnic Relations in Asia and the Pacific,* Cambridge, MIT Press, 1997, pp. 515-20.
27. For details see, Brian Michael Jenkins, *The Study of Terrorism: Definitional Problems,* CA: RAND
28. For details see, Walter Laqueur, *The Age of Terrorism,* London, Little Brown, 1987, pp 4-8.
29. *Ibid.*, p. 9.
30. Anat Kurz, *Contemporary Trends in World Terrorism,* Tel Aviv, The Jaffee Centre for Strategic Studies, 1997, p. 2.
31. Paul Wilkinson, *Political Terrorism,* London, Macmillan, 1976, p. 13.
32. For details see, Simon and Benjamin, "America and New Terrorism: An Exchange", *Survival,* Vol. 42, No. 2, pp. 156 - 72.
33. *Ibid.*, p. 66.
34. Quoted in Dietrich Fisher, *Non-military Aspect of Security: A Systems Approach,* United Nations Institute for Disarmament and Research (UNIDIR), Aldershot: Dartmouth Publishing Company Ltd., 1993, p. 10.
35. *World commission on Environment and Development, Our Common Future,* The Brundtland Report, New York/London: Oxford University Press, 1987, p. 290.
36. This distinction is made by Dietrich Fisher, *Non Military Aspect of Security: A System* Approach, Aldeshot, 1993, pp. 21.
37. Homer Dixon, "On the Threshold: Environmental changes as causes of Acute Conflicts", *International Security,* Vol. 16, No. 2, 1991, pp. 104-14.

SUGGESTED READINGS

1. Bruce Hoffman (1998) *Inside Terrorism,* Columbia University Press, New York.
2. Debi Chatterjee (eds) (2002), *Human Rights: Theory and Practice,* South Asian Publishers, New Delhi.
3. Gokulesh Sharma (2000), *Human Rights and Legal Remedies,* Deep and Deep Publications, New Delhi.

4. Myron Weiner (1999), *The Child and the State in India*, Oxford University Press, New Delhi.

5. Narottam Gaan (2000), *Environmentl and National Security*, South Asian Publishers, New Delhi.

6. Narottam Gaan (2000), *Environmental degradation and Conflict: The Case of Bangladesh - India,* South Asian Publishers, New Delhi.

7. Promod Misra, (2000), Human *Rights: Global Issues*, Kalpaz Publications, New Delhi.

8. Samuel P. Huntington (1968), *Political Order in Changing Societies*, Yale University Press, New Haven.

9. Sridhar K. Khatri, Gert W. Kueck (eds.) (2003), **Terrorism** *in South Asia: Impact on Development and Democratic Process*, Shipra Publications, New Delhi.

10. Upendra Baxi (1994), *Child and the Law*, UNICEF, India Country Office, New Delhi.

11. Urmila Phadnis (1990), *Ethnicity and Nation building in South Asia,* Sage, New Delhi.

12. Joseph Rothschild (1981), *Ethnopolitics: Conceptual Framework*, Columbia University Press, New York.

MODEL QUESTIONS

Objective Questions (2 Marks Each)

1. What does CEDAW stand for?
2. Which provisions of the Indian Constitution provides for the Rights of the Child?
3. Mention two important functions of the UNHRC?
4. Define the term 'indigenous people'?

Short Questions (5 Marks Each)

1. Write a brief note on the Rights of the Child.
2. Write a brief note on the various steps taken by the international community to protect the rights of the refugees.

Long Questions (15 Marks Each)

1. "Terrorism has emerged as a serious challenge to the International Human Rights regime". Discuss
2. Discuss the relevance of environmental issues in the overall human rights discourse.

UNITED NATIONS CHARTER

Reproduced below is the full text of the Preamble and Articles 1 and 55 of the Charter.

ARTICLE 1

We the peoples of the United Nations determined:

to save succeeding generations from the scourge of war, which twice in our lifetime has brought untold sorrow to mankind, and

to reaffirm faith in fundamental human rights, in the dignity and worth of the human person, in the equal rights of men and women and of nations large and small, and

to establish conditions under which justice and respect for the obligations arising from treaties and other sources of international law can be maintained, and

to promote, social progress and better standards of life in larger freedom.

And for these ends

to practise tolerance and live together in peace with one another as good neighbours, and

to unite our strength to maintain international peace and security, and

to ensure, by the acceptance of principles and the institution of methods, that armed force shall not be used, save in the common interest, and

to employ international machinery for the promotion of the economic and social advancement of all peoples,

Have resolved to combine our efforts to accomplish this aim

Accordingly, our respective Governments, through representatives assembled in the city of San Francisco, who have exhibited their full powers found to be in good, and due form, have agreed to the present Charter of the United Nations and do hereby establish an international organization to be known as the United Nations.

ARTICLE - 1

1. To maintain international peace and security, and to that end: to take effective collective measures for the prevention and removal of threats to the peace, and for the suppression of acts of aggression or other breaches of the peace, and to bring about by peaceful means, and in conformity with the principles of justice and international law, adjustment or settlement of international disputes or situations which might lead to a breach of the peace;
2. To develop friendly relations among nations based on respect for the principle of equal rights and self-determination of peoples, and to take other appropriate measures to strengthen universal peace;
3. To achieve international cooperation in solving international problems of an economic, social, cultural, or humanitarian character, and in promoting and encouraging respect for human rights and for fundamental freedoms for all without distinction as to race, sex, language, or religion; and
4. To be a centre for harmonizing the actions of nations in the attainment of these common ends.

ARTICLE - 55

With a view to the creation of conditions of stability and well-being which are necessary for peaceful and friendly relations among nations based on respect for the principle of equal rights and self-determination of peoples, the United Nations shall promote:

a. higher standards of living, full employment, and conditions of economic and social progress and development;
b. Solutions of international economic, social, health, and related problems; and international cultural and educational cooperation; and
c. Universal respect for, and observance of, human rights and fundamental freedoms for all without distinction as to race, sex, language, or religion.

APPENDIX B

UNIVERSAL DECLARATION OF HUMAN RIGHTS

On 10 December 1948, the General Assembly of the United Nations adopted and proclaimed the **Universal Declaration of Human Rights.** The list of Human Rights elaborated in the **Declaration** provides a common standard of 'achievement for all peoples land all nations'. Considering the world-wide historic significance of this **Declaration,** the full text of which is reproduced below, 10 December is observed as the World Human Rights Day every year.

PREAMBLE

Whereas recognition of the inherent dignity and of the equal and inalienable rights of all members of the human family is the foundation of freedom, justice and peace in the world.

Whereas disregard and contempt for human rights have resulted in barbarous acts which have outraged the conscience of mankind, and the advent of a world in which human beings shall enjoy freedom of speech and belief and freedom from fear and want has been proclaimed as the highest aspiration of the common people.

Whereas it is essential, if man is not to be compelled to have recourse, as a last resort, to rebellion against tyranny and oppression, that human rights should be protected by the rule of law.

Whereas it is essential to promote the development of friendly relations between nations.

Whereas the peoples of the United Nations have in the Charter reaffirmed their faith in fundamental human rights, in the dignity and worth of the human person and in the equal rights of men and women and have determined to promote social progress and better standards of life in larger freedom.

Whereas Member States have pledged themselves to achieve, in cooperation with the United Nations, the promotion of universal respect for and observance of human rights and fundamental freedoms.

Whereas a common understanding of these rights and freedoms is of the greatest importance for the full realization of this pledge,

The General Assembly

Proclaims this Universal Declaration of Human Rights as a common standard of achievement for all peoples and all nations, to the end that every individual and every organ of society, keeping this Declaration constantly in mind, shall strive by teaching and education to promote respect for these rights and freedoms and by progressive measures, national and international, to secure their universal and effective recognition and observance, both among the peoples of Member States themselves and among the peoples of territories under their jurisdiction.

Article - 1

All human beings are born free and equal in dignity and rights. They are endowed with reason and conscience and should act towards one another in a spirit of brotherhood.

Article - 2

Everyone is entitled to all the rights and freedoms set forth in this Declaration, without distinction of any kind, such as race, colour, sex, language, religion, political or other opinion, national or social origin, property, birth or other status. Furthermore, no distinction shall be made on the basis of the political, jurisdictional or international status of the country or territory to which a person belongs, whether it be independent, trust, non-self-government or under any other limitation of sovereignty.

Article - 3

Everyone has the right to life, liberty and security of person.

Article - 4

No one shall be held in slavery or servitude; slavery and the slave trade shall be prohibited in all their forms.

Article - 5

No one shall be subjected to torture or to cruel, inhuman or degrading treatment or punishment.

Article - 6

Everyone has the right to recognition everywhere as a person before the law.

Article - 7

All are equal before the law and are entitled without any discrimination to equal protection of the law. All are entitled to equal protection against any discrimination in violation of this Declaration and against any incitement to such discrimination.

Article - 8

Everyone has the right to an effective remedy by the competent national tribunals for acts violating the fundamental rights granted him by the constitution or by law.

Article - 9

No one shall be subjected to arbitrary arrest, detention or exile.

Article - 10

Everyone is entitled in full equality to a fair and public hearing by an independent and impartial tribunal, in the determination of his rights and obligations and of any criminal charge against him.

Article - 11

1. Everyone charged with a penal offence has the right to be presumed innocent until proved guilty according to law in a public trial at which he has had all the guarantees necessary for his defence.

2. No one shall be held guilty of any penal offence on account of any act or omission which does not constitute a penal offence, under national or international law, at the time when it was committed. Nor shall a heavier penalty be imposed than the one that was applicable at the time the penal offence was committed.

Article - 12

No one shall be subjected to arbitrary interference with his privacy, family, home or correspondence, nor to attacks upon his honour and reputation. Everyone has the right to the protection of the law against such interference or attacks.

Article - 13

1. Everyone has the right to freedom of movement and residence within the borders of each State.
2. Everyone has the right to leave any country, including his own, and to return to his country.

Article - 14

1. Everyone has the right to seek and to enjoy in other countries asylum from persecution.
2. This right may not be invoked in the case of prosecutions genuinely arising from non-political crimes or from acts contrary to the purposes land principles of the United Nations.

Article - 15

1. Everyone has the right to a nationality.
2. No one shall be arbitrarily deprived of his nationality nor denied the right to change his nationality.

Article - 16

1. Men and women of full age, without any limitation due to race, nationality or religion, have the right to marry and to found a family. They are entitled to equal rights as to marriage, during marriage and at its dissolution.
2. Marriage shall be entered into only with the free and full consent of the intending spouses.
3. The family is the natural and fundamental group unit of society and is entitled to protection by society and the State.

Article - 17

1. Everyone has the right to own property alone as well as in association with others.

2. No one shall be arbitrarily deprived of his property.

Article - 18

Everyone has the right to freedom of thought, conscience and religion; this right includes freedom to change his religion or belief, and freedom, either alone or in community with others and in public or private, to manifest his religion or belief in teaching, practice, worship and observance.

Article - 19

Everyone has the right to freedom of opinion and expression; this right includes freedom to hold opinion without interference and to seek, receive and impart information and ideas through any media and regardless of frontiers.

Article - 20

1. Everyone has the right to freedom of peaceful assembly and association.
2. No one may be compelled to belong to an association.

Article - 21

1. Everyone has the right to take part in the government of his country, directly or through freely chosen representatives.
2. Everyone has the right to equal access to public services in his country.
3. The will of the people shall be the basis of the authority of government; this will shall be expressed in periodic and genuine elections which shall be by universal and equal suffrage and shall be held by secret vote or by equivalent free voting procedures.

Article - 22

Everyone, as a member of society, has the right to social security and is entitled to realization, through national effort and international cooperation and in accordance with the organization and resources of each State, of the economic, social and cultural rights indispensable for his dignity and the free development of his personality.

Article - 23

1. Everyone has the right to work, to free choice of employment, to just and favourable conditions of work and to protection against unemployment.

2. Everyone, without any discrimination, has the right to equal pay for equal work.

3. Everyone who works has the right to just and favourable remuneration ensuring for himself and his family an existence worthy of human dignity, and supplemented, if necessary, by other means of a social protection.

4. Everyone has the right to form and to join trade unions for the protection of his interests.

Article - 24

Everyone has the right to rest and leisure, including reasonable limitation of working hours and periodic holidays with pay

Article - 25

1. Everyone has the right to a standard of living adequate for the health and well-being of himself and of his family, including food, clothing, housing and medical care and necessary social services, and the right to security in the event of unemployment, sickness, disability, widowhood, old age or other lack of livelihood in circumstances beyond his control.

2. Motherhood and childhood are entitled to special care and assistance. All children, whether born in or out of wedlock, shall enjoy the same social protection.

Article - 26

1. Everyone has the right to education. Education shall be free, at least in the elementary and fundamental stages. Elementary education shall be compulsory. Technical and professional education shall be made generally available and higher education shall be equally accessible to all on the basis of merit.

2. Education shall be directed to the full development of the human personality and to the strengthening of respect for human rights and fundamental freedoms. It shall promote understanding,

tolerance and friendship among the nations, racial or religious groups, and shall further the activities of the United Nations for the maintenance of peace.

3. Parents have a prior right to choose the kind of education that shall be given to their children.

Article - 27

1. Everyone has the right freely to participate in the cultural life of the community, to enjoy the arts and to share in scientific advancement and its benefits.
2. Everyone has the right to the protection of the moral and material interests resulting from any scientific, literary or artistic production of which he is the author.

Article - 28

Everyone is entitled to a social and international order in which the rights and freedoms set forth in this Declaration can be fully realized.

Article - 29

1. Everyone has duties to the community in which alone the free and full development of his personality is possible.
2. In the exercise of his rights and freedoms, everyone shall be subject only to such limitations as are determined by law solely for the purpose of securing due recognition and respect for the rights and freedoms of others and of meeting the just requirements of morality, public order and the general welfare in a democratic society.
3. These rights and freedoms may in no case be exercised contrary to the purposes and principles of the United Nations.

Article - 30

Nothing in this Declaration be interpreted as implying for any State, group of person any right to engage in any activity or to perform any act aimed at the destruction of any of the rights and freedoms set forth herein.

APPENDIX C

INTERNATIONAL COVENANT ON ECONOMIC, SOCIAL AND CULTURAL RIGHTS

The **Universal Declaration of Human Rights** provided the basis for the formulation by the United Nations of covenant and conventions, declarations and recommendations on specific aspects. The two broad sets of Human Rights affirmed in the **Universal Declaration** - civil and political rights, and economic, social and cultural rights were elaborated and divided into two covenants - the **International Covenant on Economic, Social and Cultural Rights,** and the **International Covenant on Civil and Political Rights.** These three documents - **the Universal Declaration of Human Rights, the International Covenant on Civil and Political Rights,** and the **International Covenant on Economic, Social and Cultural Rights** - along with two protocols - the **Optional Protocol to the International Covenant on Civil and Political Rights,** -and the **Second Optional Protocol to the International Covenant on Civil and Political Rights, aiming at the Abolition of the Death Penalty** - constitute the **International Bill of Human Rights.** These are the fundamental documents which lay the basis for the protection and prmotion of human rights throughout the world. Excerpts from this **Covenant,** which was adopted by the General Assembly of the United Nations on 16 December 1966 and came into force on 3 January 1976, are reproduced below.

PREAMBLE

The States Parties to the present Covenant,

Considering that, in accordance with the principles proclaimed in the Charter of the United Nations, recognition of the inherent dignity and of the equal and inalienable rights of all members of the human family is the foundation of freedom, justice and peace in the world.

Recognizing that, these rights derive from the inherent dignity of the human person.

Recognizing that, in accordance with the Universal Declaration of Human Rights, the ideal of free human beings enjoying freedom from fear and want can only be achieved if conditions are created whereby everyone may enjoy his economic, social and cultural rights, as well as his civil and political rights.

Considering the obligation of States under the Charter of the United Nations to promote universal respect for, and observance of, human rights and freedoms.

Realizing that the individual, having duties to other individuals land to the community to which he belongs, is under a responsibility to strive for the promotion and observance of the rights recognized in the present Covenant.

Agree upon the following Articles:

PART - I

Article - 1

1. All peoples have the right of self-determination. By virtue of that right they freely determine their political status and freely pursue their economic, social and cultural development.
2. All peoples may, for their own ends, freely dispose of their natural wealth and resources without prejudice to any obligations arising out of international economic cooperation, based upon the principle of mutual benefit, and international law. In no case may a people be deprived of its own means of subsistence.

PART - 2

Article - 2

1. Each State Party to the present Covenant undertakes to take steps, individually and through international assistance and cooperation, especially economic and technical, to the maximum of its available resources, with a view to achieving progressively the full realization of the rights recognized in the present Covenant by all appropriate means, including particularly the adoption of legislative measures.
2. The States Parties to the present Covenant undertake to guarantee that the rights enunciated in the present Covenant will be exercised without discrimination of any kind as to race, colour, sex, language,

religion, political or other opinion, national or social origin, property, birth or other status.

3. Developing countries, with due regard to human rights and their national economy, may determine to what extent they would guarantee the economic rights recognized in the present Covenant to non-nationals.

Article - 3

The States Parties to the present Covenant undertake to ensure the equal right of men and women to the enjoyment of all economic, social and cultural rights set forth in the present Covenant.

Article - 4

The States Parties to the present Covenant recognize that, in the enjoyment of those rights provided by the State in conformity with the present Covenant, the State may subject such rights only to such limitations as are determined by law only in so far as this may be compatible with the nature of these rights and solely for the purpose of promoting the general welfare in a democratic society.

PART - 3

Article - 6

1. The States Parties to the present covenant recognize the right to work, which includes the right of everyone to the opportunity to gain his living by work which he freely chooses or accepts, and will take appropriate steps to safeguard this right.

2. The steps to be taken by a State Party to the present Covenant to achieve the full realization of this right shall include technical and vocational guidance and training programmes, policies and techniques to achieve steady economic, social and cultural development and full and productive employment under conditions safeguarding fundamental political and economic freedoms to the individual.

Article - 7

The States Parties to the present Covenant recognize the right of everyone to the enjoyment of just and favourable conditions of work, which ensure, in particular:

a. Remuneration which provides all workers, as a minimum, with:

   i. Fair wages and equal remuneration for work of equal value without distinction of any kind, in particular women being guaranteed conditions of work not inferior to those enjoyed by men, with equal pay for equal work:

   ii. A decent living for themselves and their families in accordance with the provisions of the present Covenant;

b. Safe and healthy working conditions;

c. Equal opportunity for everyone to be promoted in his employment to an appropriate higher level, subject to no considerations other than those of seniority and competence;

d. Rest, leisure and reasonable limitation of working hours and periodic holidays with pay, as well as remuneration for public holidays.

Article - 8

1. The States Parties to the present Covenant undertake to ensure:

   a. The right of everyone to form trade union and join the trade union of his choice, subject only to the rules of the organization concerned, for the promotion and protection of his economic and social interests.

   b. The right of trade unions to establish national federations or confederations and the right of the latter to form or join international trade union organizations.

   c. The right of trade unions to function freely subject to no limitations other than those prescribed by law and which are necessary in a democratic society in the interests of national security or public order or for the protection of the rights and freedoms of others.

   d. The right to strike, provided that it is exercised in conformity with the laws of the particular country.

Article - 9

The States Parties to the present Covenant recognize the right of everyone to social security, including social insurance.

Article - 10

The States Parties to the present Covenant recognize that:

1. The widest possible protection and assistance should be accorded to the family, which is the natural fundamental group unit of society, particularly for its establishment and while it is responsible for the care and education of dependent children. Marriage must be entered into with the free consent of the intending spouses.
2. Special protection should be accorded to mothers during a reasonable period before and after childbirth. During such period working mother should be accorded paid leave or leave with adequate social security benefits.
3. Special measures of protection and assistance should be taken on behalf of all children and young persons without any discrimination for reasons of parentage or other conditions. Children and young persons should be protected from economic and social exploitation. Their employment in work harmful to their morals or health or dangerous to life or likely to hamper their normal development should be punishable by law. States should also set age limits below which the paid employment of child labour should be prohibited and punishable by law.

Article - 11

1. The States Parties to the present Covenant recognize the right of everyone to an adequate standard of living for himself and his family, including adequate food, clothing and housing, and to the continuous improvement of living conditions. The States Parties will take appropriate steps to ensure the realization of this right, recognizing to this effect the essential importance of international cooperation based on free consent.
2. The States Parties to the present Covenant, recognizing the fundamental right of everyone to be free from hunger, shall take, individually and through international cooperation, the measures, including specific programmes, which are needed:

   a. To improve methods of production, conservation and distribution of food by making full use of technical and scientific knowledge, by disseminating knowledge of the principles of nutrition and by developing or reforming agrarian systems in such a way as to achieve the most efficient development and utilization of natural resources;

b. Taking into account the problems for both food-importing and food-exporting countries, to ensure an equitable distribution of world food supplies in relation to need.

Article - 12

1. The States Parties to the present Covenant recognize the right of everyone to the enjoyment of the highest attainable standard of physical and mental health.

2. The steps to be taken by the States Parties to the present Covenant to achieve the full realization of this right shall include those necessary for:

   a. The provision for the reduction of the stillbirth-rate and of infant mortality and for the healthy development of the child;

   b. The improvement of all aspects of environmental and industrial hygiene;

   c. The prevention, treatment and control of epidemic, endemic, occupational and other diseases;

   d. The creation of conditions which would assure to all medical service and medical attention in the event of sickness.

Article - 13

1. The States Parties to the present Covenant recognize the right of everyone to education. They agree that education shall be directed to the full development of the human personality and the sense of its dignity, and shall strengthen the respect for human rights and fundamental freedoms. They further agree that education shall enable all persons to participate effectively in a free society, promote understanding, tolerance and friendship among all nations and all racial, ethnic or religious groups, and further the activities of the United Nations for the maintenance of peace.

2. The States Parties to the present Covenant recognize that, with a view to achieving the full realization of this right:

   a. Primary education shall be compulsory and available free to all;

b. Secondary education in its different forms, including technical and vocational secondary education, shall be made generally available and accessible to all by every appropriate means, and in particular by the progressive introduction of free education;

c. Higher education shall be made equally accessible to all, on the basis of capacity, by every appropriate means, and in particular by the progressive introduction of free education;

d. Fundamental education shall be encouraged or intensified as far as possible for those persons who have not received or completed the whole period of their primary education;

e. The development of a system of schools at all levels shall be actively pursued, and adequate fellowship system shall be established, and the material conditions of teaching staff shall be continuously improved.

3. The States Parties to the present Covenant undertake to have respect for the liberty of parents and, when applicable, legal guardians to choose for their children schools, other than those established by the public authorities, which conform to such minimum educational standards as may be laid down or approved by the State and to ensure the religious and moral education of their children in conformity with their own convictions.

4. No part of this Article shall be construed so as to interfere with the liberty of individuals and bodies to establish and direct educational institutions, subject always to the observance of the principles set forth in paragraph 1 of this Article and to lthe requirement that the education given in such institutions shall conform to such minimum standards as may be laid down by the State.

Article - 15

1. The States Parties to the present Covenant recognize the right of everyone:

   a. To take part in cultural life;

   b. To enjoy the benefits of scientific progress and its applications;

   c. To benefit from the protection of the moral and material interests resulting from any scientific, literary or artistic production of which he is the author.

2. The steps to be taken by the States Parties to the present Covenant to achieve the full realization of this right shall include those necessary for the conservation, the development and the diffusion of science and culture.

3. The States Parties to the present Covenant undertake to respect the freedom indispensable for scientific research and creative activity.

4. The States Parties to the present Covenant recognize the benefits to be derived from the encouragement and development of international contacts and cooperation in the scientific and culture fields.

APPENDIX D

INTERNATIONAL COVENANT ON CIVIL AND POLITICAL RIGHTS

Reproduced below are excerpts from the **International Covenant on Civil and Political Rights** which was adopted by the General Assembly of the United Nations on 16 December 1966 and came into force on 23 March 1976.

PREAMBLE

The States Parties to the Present Covenant

Considering that, in accordance with the principles proclaimed in the Charter of the United Nations, recognition of the inherent dignity and of the equal and inalienable rights of all members of the human family is the foundation of freedom, justice and peace in the world.

Recognizing that these rights derive from the inherent dignity of the human person.

Recognizing that, in accordance with the Universal Declaration of Human Rights, the ideal of free human beings enjoying civil and political freedom and freedom from fear and want can only be achieved if conditions are created whereby everyone may enjoy his civil and political rights, as well as his economic, social and cultural rights,

Considering the obligation of States under the Charter of the United Nations to promote universal respect for, and observance of human rights and freedoms.

Realizing that the individual, having duties to other individuals and to the community to which he belongs, is under a responsibility to strive for the promotion and observance of the rights recognized in the present Covenant.

Agree upon the following Articles:

PART - I

Article - 1

1. All peoples have the right of self-determination. By virtue of that right they freely determine their political status and freely pursue their economic, social and cultural development.
2. All peoples may, for their own ends, freely dispose of their natural wealth and resources without prejudice to any obligations arising out of international economic cooperation based upon the principle of mutual benefit, and international law. In no case may a people be deprived of its own means of subsistence.
3. The States Parties to the present Covenant, including those having responsibility for the administration of Non-Self-Governing and Trust Territories, shall promote the realization of the right of self-determination, and shall respect the right, in conformity with the provisions of the Charter of the United Nations.

PART - 2

Article - 2

1. Each State Party to the present Covenant undertakes to respect and to ensure to all individuals within its territory and subject to its jurisdiction the rights recognized in the present Covenant, without distinction of any kind, such as race, colour, sex, language, religion, political or other opinion, national or social origin, property, birth or other status.

2. Where not already provided for by existing legislative or other measures, each State Party to the present Covenant undertakes to take the necessary steps, in accordance with its constitutional processes and with the provisions of the present Covenant, to adopt such legislative or other measures as may be necessary to give effect to the rights recognized in the present Covenant.

3. Each State Party to the present Covenant undertakes:
   a. To ensure that any person whose rights or freedoms as herein recognized are violated shall have an effective remedy, notwithstanding that the violation has been committed by persons acting in an official capacity;

b. To ensure that any person claiming such a remedy shall have his right thereto determined by competent, judicial, administrative or legislative authorities, or by any other competent authority provided for by the legal system of the State, and to develop the possibilities of judicial remedy;

Article - 3

The States Parties to the present Covenant undertake to ensure the equal right of men and women to the enjoyment of all civil and political rights set forth in the present Covenant.

Article - 4

1. In time of public emergency which threatens the life of the nation and the existence of which is officially proclaimed, the States Parties to the present Covenant may take measures derogating from their obligations under the present Covenant to the extent strictly required by the exigencies of the situation, provided that such measures are not inconsistent with their other obligations under international law and do not involve discrimination solely on the ground of race, colour, sex, language, religion or social origin.

PART - 3

Article - 6

1. Every human being has the inherent right to life. This right shall be protected by law. No one shall be arbitrarily deprived of his life.

2. In countries which have not abolished the death penalty, sentence of death may be imposed only for the most serious crimes in accordance with the law in force at the time of the commission of the crime and not contrary to the provisions of the present Covenant and to the Convention on the Prevention and Punishment of the Crime of Genocide.

3. Anyone sentenced to death shall have the right to seek pardon or commutation of the sentence. Amnesty, pardon or commutation of the sentence of death may be granted in all cases.

4. Sentence of death shall not be imposed for crimes committed by persons below eighteen years of age and shall not be carried out on pregnant women.

Article - 7

1. No one shall be subjected to torture or to cruel, inhuman or degrading treatment or punishment. In particular, no one shall be subjected without his free consent to medical or scientific experimentation.

Article - 8

1. No one shall be held in slavery; slavery and the slave trade in all their forms shall be prohibited.
2. No one shall be held in servitude.
3. No one shall be required to perform forced or compulsory labour.

Article - 9

1. Everyone has the right to liberty and security of person. No one shall be subjected to arbitrary arrest or detention. No one shall be deprived of his liberty except on such grounds and in accordance with such procedure as are established by law.
2. Anyone who is arrested shall be informed, at the time of arrest, of the reasons for his arrest and shall be promptly informed of any charges against him.
3. Anyone arrested or detained on a criminal charge shall be brought promptly before a judge or other officer authorized by law to exercise judicial power and shall be entitled to trial within a reasonable time or to release.
4. Anyone who is deprived of his liberty by arrest or detention shall be entitled to take proceedings before a court, in order that court may decide without delay, on the lawfulness of his detention and order his release if the detention is not lawful.
5. Anyone who has been the victim of unlawful arrest or detention shall have an enforceable right to compensation.

Article - 10

1. All persons deprived of their liberty shall be treated with humanity and with respect for the inherent dignity of the human person.

2. a. Accused persons shall, save in exceptional circumstances, be segregated from convicted persons and shall be subject to separate treatment appropriate to their status as unconvicted persons;

   b. Accused juvenile persons shall be separated from adults and brought as speedily as possible for adjudication.

3. The penitentiary system shall comprise treatment of prisoners the essential aim of which shall be their reformation and social rehabilitation. Juvenile offenders shall be segregated from adults and be accorded treatment appropriate to their age and legal status.

Article - 12

1. Everyone lawfully within the territory of a State shall, within that territory, have the right to liberty of movement and freedom to choose his residence.
2. Everyone shall be free to leave any country, including his own.
3. The above-mentioned rights shall not be subject to any restrictions except those which are provided by law, are necessary to protect national security, public order, public health or morals or the rights and freedoms of others, and are consistent with the other rights recognized in the present Covenant.
4. No one shall be arbitrarily deprived of the right to enter his own country.

Article - 14

1. All persons shall be equal before the courts and tribunals. In the determination of any criminal charge against him, or of his rights and obligations in a suit at law, everyone shall be entitled to a fair and public hearing by a competent, independent and impartial tribunal established by law.
2. Everyone charged with a criminal offence shall have the right to be presumed innocent until proved guilty according to law.
3. In the determination of any criminal charge against him, everyone shall be entitled to the following minimum guarantees, in full equality:

a. To be informed promptly and in detail in a language which he understands of the nature and cause of the charge against him;

b. To have adequate time and facilities for the preparation of his defence and to communicate with counsel of his own choosing;

c. To be tried without undue delay;

d. To be tried in his present, and to defend himself in person or through legal assistance of his own choosing.

e. Not to be compelled to testify against himself or to confess guilt.

4. In the case of juvenile persons, the procedure shall be such as will take account of their age and the desirability of promoting their rehabilitation.

Article - 16

Everyone shall have the right to recognition everywhere as a person before the law.

Article - 17

1. No one shall be subjected to arbitrary or unlawful interference with his privacy, family, home or correspondence, nor to unlawful attacks on his honour and reputation.

2. Everyone has the right to the protection of the law against such interference or attacks.

Article - 18

1. Everyone shall have the right to freedom of thought, conscience and religion. This right shall include freedom to have or to adopt a religion or belief of his choice, and freedom, either individually or in community with others and in public or private, to manifest his religion or belief in worship, observance, practice and teaching.

2. No one shall be subject to coercion which would impair his freedom to have or to adopt a religion or belief of his choice.

3. Freedom to manifest one's religion or beliefs may b subject only to such limitations as are prescribed by law and are necessary to

protect public safety, order, health, or morals or the fundamental rights and freedoms of other.

4. The States Parties to the present Covenant undertake to have respect for the liberty of parents and, when applicable, legal guardians to ensure the religious and moral education of their children in conformity with their own convictions.

Article - 19

1. Everyone shall have the right to hold opinions without interference.

2. Everyone shall have the right to freedom of expression; this right shall include freedom to seek, receive and impart information and ideas of all kinds, regardless of frontiers, either orally, in writing or in print, in the form of art, or through any other media of his choice.

3. The exercise of the rights provided for in paragraph 2 of this Article carries with it special duties and responsibilities. It may therefore be subject to certain restrictions, but these shall only be such as are provided by law and are necessary.

   a. For respect of the rights or reputations of others;

   b. For the protection of national security or of public order *(ordre public)*, or of public health or morals.

Article - 20

1. Any propaganda for war shall be prohibited by law.

2. Any advocacy of national, racial or religious hatred that constitutes incitement to discrimination, hostility or violence shall be prohibited by law.

Article - 21

The right of peaceful assembly shall be recognized. No, restrictions may be placed on the exercise of this right other than those imposed in conformity with the law and which are necessary in a democratic society in the interests of national security or public safety, public order (*ordre public*), the protection of public health or morals or the protection of the rights and freedoms of others.

Article - 22

1. Everyone shall have the right to freedom of association with others, including the right to form and join trade unions for the protection of his interests.

Article - 23

1. The family is the natural and fundamental group unit of society and is entitled to protection by society and the State.
2. The right of men and women of marriageable age to marry and to found a family shall be recognized.
3. No marriage shall be entered into without the free and full consent of the intending spouses.
4. States Parties to the present Covenant shall take appropriate steps to ensure equality of rights and responsibilities of spouses as to marriage, during marriage and at its dissolution. In the case of dissolution, provision shall be made for the necessary protection of any children.

Article - 24

1. Every child shall have, without any discrimination as to race, colour, sex, language, religion, national or social origin, property or birth, the right to such measures of protection as are required by his status as a minor, on the part of his family, society and the State.
2. Every child shall be registered immediately after birth and shall have a name.
3. Every child has the right to acquire a nationality.

Article - 25

Every citizen shall have the right and the opportunity, without any of the distinctions mentioned in Article 2 and without unreasonable restrictions:

a. To take part in the conduct of public affairs, directly or through freely chosen representatives;

b. To vote and to be elected at genuine periodic elections which shall be by universal and equal suffrage and shall be held by secret ballot, guaranteeing the free expressions of the will of the electors;

c. To have access, on general terms of equality, to public service in his country.

Article - 26

All persons are equal before the law and are entitled without any discrimination to the equal protection of the law. In this respect, the law shall prohibit any discrimination and guarantee to all persons equal and effective protection against discrimination on any ground such as race, colour, sex, language, religion, political or other opinion, national or social origin, property, birth or other status.

Article - 27

In those States in which ethnic, religious or linguistic minorities exist, persons belonging to such minorities shall not be denied the right, in community with the other member so their group, to enjoy their own culture, to profess and practise their own religion, or to use their own language.

PART - 4

ARTICLE - 40

1. The States Parties to the present Covenant undertake to submit reports on the measures they have adopted which give effect to the rights recognized herein and on the progress made in the enjoyment of those rights.

APPENDIX E

CONVENTION ON THE ELIMINATION OF ALL FORMS OF DISCRIMINATION AGAINST WOMEN

This Convention was adopted by the General Assembly of he United Nations on 18 December 1979 and came into force on 3 September 1981. Excerpts from the Convention are reproduced below.

The States Parties to the present Convention.

Noting that the Charter of the United reaffirms faith in fundamental human rights, in the dignity and worth of the human person and in the equal rights of men and women.

Noting that the Universal Declaration of Human Rights affirms the principle of the inadmissibility of discrimination and proclaims that all human beings are born free and equal in dignity and rights and that everyone is entitled to all the rights and freedoms set forth therein, without distinction of any kind, including distinction based on sex,

Noting that the States Parties to the International Covenants on Human Rights have the obligation to ensure the equal rights of men and women to enjoy all economic, social, cultural, civil and political rights,

Considering the international conventions concluded under the auspices of the United Nations and the specialized agencies promoting equally of rights of men and women.

Noting also the resolutions, declarations and recommendations adopted by the United Nations and the specialized agencies promoting equality of rights of men and women.

Concerned, however, that despite these various instruments extensive discrimination against women continues to exist.

Recalling that discrimination against women violates the principles of equality of rights and respect for human dignity, is an obstacle to the participation of women, on equal terms with men, in the political, social, economic and cultural life of their countries, hampers the growth of the prosperity of society and the family and makes more difficult the full development of the potentialities of women in the service of their countries and of humanity,

Concerned that in situations of poverty women have the least access to food, health, education, training and opportunities for employment and other needs,

Convinced that the establishment of the new international economic order based on equity and justice will contribute significantly towards the promotion of equality between men and women.

Emphasizing that the eradication of *apartheid,* all forms of racism, racial discrimination, colonialism, neo-colonialism, aggression, foreign occupation and domination and interference in the internal affairs of States is essential to the full enjoyment of the right of men and women.

Affirming that the strengthening of international peace and security, the relaxation of international tension, mutual cooperation among all States irrespective of their social and economic systems, general and complete disarmament, in particular nuclear disarmament under strict and effective international control, the affirmation of the principles of justice, equality and mutual benefit in relations among counties and the realization of the right of people under alien and colonial domination and foreign occupation to self-determination and independence, as well as respect for national sovereignty and territorial integrity, will promote social progress and development and as a consequence will contribute to the attainment of full equality between men and women.

Convinced that the full and complete development of a country, the welfare of the world land the cause of peace require the maximum participation of women on equal terms with men in all fields,

Bearing in mind the great contribution of women to the welfare of the family and to the development of society, so far not fully recognized, the social significance of maternity and the role of both parents in the family and in the upbringing of children, and aware that the role of women in procreation should not be a basis for discrimination but that the upbringing of children requires a sharing of responsibility between men and women and society as a whole.

Aware that a change in the traditional role of men as well as the role of women in society and in the family is needed to achieve full equality between men and women.

Determined to implement the principles set forth in the Declaration on the Elimination of Discrimination against Women and, for that purpose, to adopt the measures required for the elimination of such discrimination in all its forms and manifestations,

Have agreed on the following :

PART - 1

Article - 1

For the purposes of the present Convention, the term discrimination against women shall mean any distinction, exclusion or restriction made on the basis of sex which has the effect or purpose of impairing or nullifying the recognition, enjoyment or exercise by women, irrespective of their marital status, on a basis of equality of men and women, of human rights and fundamental freedoms in the political, economic, social, cultural, civil or any other field.

Article - 2

States Parties condemn discrimination against women in all its forms, agree to pursue by all appropriate means and without delay a policy of eliminating discrimination against women and to this end undertake:

a. to embody the principle of the equality of men and women in their national constitutions or other appropriate legislation if not yet incorporated therein and to ensure, through law and other appropriate means, the practical realization of this principle;

b. to adopt appropriate legislative and other measures, including sanctions where appropriate, prohibiting all discrimination against women;

c. to establish legal protection of the rights of women on an equal basis with men and to ensure through competent national tribunals and other public institutions the effective protection of women against any act of discrimination;

d. to refrain from engaging in any act or practice of discrimination against women and to ensure that public authorities and institutions shall act in conformity with this obligation;

e. to take all appropriate measures to eliminate discrimination against women by any person, organization or enterprise;

f. to take all appropriate measures, including legislation, to modify or abolish existing laws, regulations, customs and practices which constitute discrimination against women '

g. to repeal all national penal provisions which constitute discrimination against women.

Article - 3

States Parties shall take in al fields, in particular in the political, social, economic and cultural fields, all appropriate measures, including legislation, to ensure the full development and advancement of women, for the purpose of guaranteeing them the exercise and enjoyment of human rights and fundamental freedoms on a basis of equality with men.

Article - 4

1. Adoption by States Parties of temporary special measures aimed at accelerating de facto equality between men and women shall not be considered discrimination as defined in the present convention, but shall in no way entail as a consequence the maintenance of unequal or separate standards; these measures shall be discontinued when the objectives of equality of opportunity and treatment have been achieved.

2. Adoption by States Parties of special measures, including those measures contained in the present convention, aimed at protecting maternity shall not be considered discriminatory.

Article - 5

States Parties shall take all appropriate measures:

a. to modify the social and cultural patterns of conduct of men and women, with a view to achieving the elimination of prejudices and customary and all other practices which are based on the idea of the inferiority or the superiority of either of the sexes or on stereotyped roles for men and women;

b. to ensure that family education includes a proper understanding of maternity as a social function and the recognition of the common responsibility of men and women in the upbringing and development of their children, it being understood that the interest of the children is the primordial consideration in all cases.

Article - 6

States Parties shall take all appropriate measures, including legislation, to suppress all forms of traffic in women and exploitation of prostitution of women.

PART - 2

Article - 7

States Parties shall take all appropriate measures to eliminate discrimination against women in the political and public life of the country and, in particular, shall ensure to women, on equal terms with men, the Right;

a. to vote in all elections and public referenda and to be eligible for elections to all publicly elected bodies;

b. to participate in the formulation of government policy and the implementation thereof and to hold public office and perform all public functions at all levels of government;

c. to participate in non-governmental organizations and association concerned with the public and political life of the country.

Article - 8

States Parties shall take all appropriate measures to ensure to women, on equal terms with men and without any discrimination, the opportunity to represent their Governments at the international level and to participate in the work of international organizations.

Article - 9

1. States Parties shall grant women equal rights with men to acquire, change or retain their nationality. They shall ensure in particular that neither marriage to an alien nor change of nationality by the husband during marriage shall automatically change the nationality of the wife, render her stateless or force upon her the nationality of the husband.

PART - 3

Article - 10

States Parties shall take all appropriate measures to eliminate discrimination against women in order to ensure to them equal rights with men in the field of education and in particular to ensure, on a basis of equality of men and women:

a. the same conditions for career and vocational guidance for access to studies and for the achievement of diplomas in educational establishments of all categories in rural as well as in urban areas; this equality shall be ensured in pre-school, general, technical, professional and higher technical education, as well as in all types of vocational training.

b. Access to the same curricula, the same examinations, teaching staff with qualifications of the same standard and school premises and equipment of the same quality;

c. The elimination of any stereotyped concept of the roles of men and women at all levels and in all forms of education by encouraging coeducation and other types of education which will help to achieve this aim and in particular, by the revision of textbooks and school programmes and the adaptation of teaching methods,

d. The same opportunities to benefit from scholarships and other study grants;

e. The same opportunities for access to programmes of continuing education, including adult functional literacy programmes, particularly those aimed at reducing, at the earliest possible time, any gap in education existing between men and women;

f. The reduction of female student drop-our rates and the organization of programmes for girls and women who have left school prematurely;

g. The same opportunities to participate actively in sports and physical education;

h. Access to specific educational information to help to ensure the health and well-being of families, including information and advice on family planning.

Article - 11

1. States Parties shall take all appropriate measures to eliminate discrimination against women in the field of employment in order to ensure, on a basis of equality of men and women, the same rights, in particular;

   a. The right to work as an inalienable right of all human beings;

   b. The right to the same employment opportunities; including the application of the same criteria for selection in matters of employment;

   c. The right to free choice of profession and employment, the right to promotion, job security and all benefits and conditions of service and the right to receive vocational training and retraining, including apprenticeships, advanced vocational training and recurrent training.

   d. The right to equal remuneration, including benefits, and to equal treatment in respect of work of equal value, as well as equality of treatment in the evaluation of the quality of work;

   e. The right to social security, particularly in cases of retirement, unemployment, sickness, invalidity and old age and other incapacity to work, as well as the right to paid leave;

   f. The right to protection of health and to safety in working conditions, including the safeguarding of the function of reproduction.

2. In order to prevent discrimination against women on the grounds of marriage or maternity and to ensure their effective right to work, States Parties shall take appropriate measures:

   a. To prohibit, subject to the imposition of sanctions, dismissal on the grounds of pregnancy or of maternity leave and discrimination in dismissals on the basis of marital status;

   b. To introduce maternity leave with pay or with comparable social benefits without loss of former employment, seniority or social allowances;

   c. To encourage the provision of the necessary supporting social services to enable parents to combine family obligations with work responsibilities and participation in public life, in particular through promoting the establishment and development of a network of child-care facilities;

d. To provide special protection to women during pregnancy in types of work proved to be harmful to them.

3. Protective legislation relating to matters covered in this Article shall be reviewed periodically in the light of scientific and technological knowledge and shall be revised, repealed or extended as necessary.

Article - 12

1. States Parties shall take all appropriate measures to eliminate discrimination against women in the field of health care in order to ensure, on a basis of equality of men and women, access to health care services, including those related to family planning.

2. Notwithstanding the provisions of paragraph 1 of this Article, States Parties shall ensure to women appropriate services in connection with pregnancy, confinement and the post-natal period, granting free services where necessary, as well as adequate nutrition during pregnancy and lactation.

Article - 14

1. States Parties shall take into account the particular problems faced by rural women and the significant roles which rural women play in the economic survival of their families, including their work in the non-monetized sectors of the economy, and shall take all appropriate measures to ensure the application of the provisions of the present Convention to women in rural areas.

2. States Parties shall take all appropriate measures to eliminate discrimination against women in rural areas in order to ensure, on a basis of equality of men and women, that they participate in and benefit from rural development and, in particular, shall ensure to such women the right:

   a. To participate in the elaboration and implementation of development planning at all levels;

   b. To have access to adequate health care facilities, including information, counselling and services in family planning;

c. To benefit directly from social security programmes;

d. To obtain all types of training and education, formal and non-formal, including that relating to functional literacy, as well as, inter alia, the benefit of all community and extension services, in order to increase their technical proficiency;

e. To organize self-help groups and cooperatives in order to obtain equal access to economic opportunities through employment or self-employment;

f. To participate in all community activities;

g. To have access to agricultural credit and loans, marketing facilities, appropriate technology and equal treatment in land and agrarian reform as well as in land resettlement schemes;

h. To enjoy adequate living conditions, particularly in relation to housing, sanitation, electricity and water supply, transport and communications.

PART - 4

Article - 15

1. States Parties shall accord to women equality with men before the law.

Article - 16

1. States Parties shall take all appropriate measures to eliminate discrimination against women in all matters relating to marriage and family relations and in particular shall ensure, on a basis of equality of men and women.

   a. The same right to enter into marriage;

   b. The same right freely to choose a spouse and to enter into marriage only with their free and full consent;

   c. The same rights and responsibilities during marriage and at its dissolution;

   d. The same rights and responsibilities as parents, irrespective of their marital status, in matters relating to their children; in all cases the interests of the children shall be paramount;

e. The same rights to decide freely and responsibly on the number and spacing of their children and to have access to the information, education and means to enable them to exercise these rights;

f. The same rights and responsibilities with regard to guardianship, wardship, trusteeship and adoption of children, or similar institutions where these concepts exists in national legislation; in all cases the interests of the children shall be paramount;

g. The same personal rights as husband and wife, including the right to choose a family name, a profession and an occupation.

h. The same rights for both spouses in respect of the ownership, acquisition, management, administration, enjoyment and disposition of property, whether free of charge or for a valuable consideration.

2. The betrothal and the marriage of a child shall have no legal effect, and all necessary action, including legislation, shall be taken to specify a minimum age for marriage and to make the registration of marriages in an official registry compulsory.

APPENDIX F

DECLARATION ON THE RIGHT TO DEVELOPMENT

A landmark development in the formulation and recognition of new human rights is the **Declaration on the Right to Development** which was adopted by the General Assembly of the United Nations on 4 December 1986. This **Declaration** is particularly significant for its importance to the developing countries even though the necessary means for enforcing it are lacking.

The text of this Declaration is reproduced below:

The General Assembly

Bearing in mind the purposes and principles of the Charter of the United Nations relating to the achievement of international co-operation in solving international problems of economic, social, cultural or humanitarian nature, and in promoting and encouraging respect for human rights and fundamental freedoms for all without distinction as to race, sex, languages or religion.

Recognizing that development is a comprehensive economic, social, cultural and political process, which aims at the constant improvement of the well-being of the entire population and of all individuals on the basis of their active, free and meaningful participation in development and in the fair distribution of benefits resulting therefrom.

Considering that under the provisions of the Universal Declaration of Human Rights everyone is entitled to a social and international order in which the rights and freedoms set forth in that Declaration can be fully realized.

Recalling the provisions of the International Covenant of Economic, Social and Cultural Rights and of the International Covenant on Civil and Political Rights,

Recalling further the relevant agreements, conventions, resolutions, recommendations and other instruments of the United Nations and its specialized agencies concerning the integral development of the human being, economic and social progress and development of all peoples, including those instruments concerning decolonization, the prevention of discrimination, respect for and observance of human rights and fundamental freedoms, the maintenance of international peace and security and the further promotion of friendly relations and cooperation among States in accordance with the Charter.

Recalling the right of peoples to self-determination, by virtue of which they have the right freely to determine their political status and to pursue their economic, social and cultural development.

Recalling also the right of peoples to exercise, subject to the relevant provisions of both International Covenants on Human Rights, full and complete sovereignty over all their natural wealth and resources.

Mindful of the obligation of States under the Charter to promote universal respect for and observance of human rights and fundamental freedoms for all without distinction of any kind such as race, colour, sex, language, religion, political or other opinion, national or social origin, property, birth or other status.

Considering that the elimination of the massive and flagrant violations of the human rights of the peoples and individuals affected by situations such as those resulting from colonialism, neo-colonialism, apartheid, all forms of racism and racial discrimination, foreign domination and occupation, aggression and threats against national sovereignty national unity and territorial integrity and threats of war would contribute to the establishment of circumstances propitious to the development of a great part of mankind.

Concerned at the existence of serious obstacles to development, as well as to the complete fulfilment of human beings and of peoples constituted, inter alia, by the denial of civil, political, economic, social and cultural rights, and considering that all human rights and fundamental freedoms are indivisible and interdependent and that, in order to promote development, equal attention and urgent consideration should be given to the implementation, promotion and protection of civil, political economic, social and cultural rights and that accordingly, the promotion of respect for and enjoyment of certain human rights and fundamental freedoms cannot justify the denial of other human rights and fundamental freedoms.

Considering that international peace and security are essential elements for the realization of the right to development.

Reaffirming that there is a close relationship between disarmament and development and that progress in the field of disarmament would considerably promote progress in the field of development and that resources released through disarmament measures should be devoted to the economic and social development and well-being of all peoples and, in particular, those of the developing countries,

Recognizing that the human person is the central subject of the development process and that development policy should therefore make the human being the main participant and beneficiary of development.

Recognizing that the creation of conditions favourable to the development of peoples and individuals is the primary responsibility of their States.

Aware that efforts at the international level to promote and protect human rights should be accompanied by efforts to establish a new international economic order.

Confirming that the right to development is an inalienable human right and that equality of opportunity for development is a prerogative both of nations and of individuals who make up nations.

Proclaims the following Declaration on the Right to Development;

Article - 1

1. The right to development is an inalienable human right by virtue of which every human person and all peoples are entitled to participate in, contribute to and enjoy economic, social, cultural and political development, in which all human rights and fundamental freedoms can be fully realized.
2. The human right to development also implies the full realization of the right of peoples to self-determination, which includes, subject to the relevant provisions of both international Covenants on Human Rights, the exercise of their inalienable right to full sovereignty over all their natural wealth and resources.

Article - 2

1. The human person is the central subject of development and should be the active participant and beneficiary of the right to development.

2. All human beings have a responsibility for development, individually and collectively, taking into account the need for full respect for their human rights and fundamental freedoms as well as their duties to the community, which alone can ensure the free and complete fulfillment of the human being and they should therefore promote and protect an appropriate political, social and economic order for development.

3. States have the right and the duty to formulate appropriate national development policies that aim at constant, improvement of the well-being of the entire population and of all individuals, on the basis of their active, free and meaningful participation in development and in the fair distribution of the benefits resulting therefrom.

Article - 3

1. States have the primary responsibility for the creation of national and international conditions favourable to the realization of the right to development.

2. The realization of the right to development requires full respect for the principles of international law concerning friendly relations and cooperation among States in accordance with the Charter of the United Nations.

3. States have the duty to cooperate with each other in ensuring development and eliminating obstacles to development. States should realize their rights and fulfill their duties in such as manner as to promote a new international economic order based on sovereign equality, interdependence, mutual interest and cooperation among all States, as well as to encourage the observance and realization of human rights.

Article - 4

1. States have the duty to take steps, individually and collectively, to formulate international development policies with a view to facilitating the full realization of the right to development.

2. Sustained action is required to promote more rapid development of developing countries. As a complement to the efforts of developing countries, effective international cooperation is essential in providing these countries with appropriate means and facilities to foster their comprehensive development.

Article - 5

States shall take resolute steps to eliminate the massive and flagrant violations of the human rights of peoples and human beings affected by situations such as those resulting from apartheid, all forms of racism and racial discrimination, colonialism, foreign domination and occupation, aggression, foreign interference and threats against national sovereignty, national unity and territorial, integrity, threats of war and refusal to recognize the fundamental right of peoples to self-determination.

Article - 6

1. All States should cooperate with a view to promoting, encouraging and strengthening universal respect for an observance of all human rights and fundamental freedoms for all without any distinction as to race, sex, language or religion.
2. All human rights and fundamental freedoms are indivisible and interdependent; equal attention and urgent consideration should be given to the implementation, promotion and protection of civil, political economic, social and cultural rights.
3. States should take steps to eliminate obstacles to development resulting from failure to observe civil and political rights, as well as economic, social and cultural rights.

Article - 7

All States should promote the establishment, maintenance and strengthening of international peace and security and, to that end, should do their utmost to achieve general and complete disarmament under effective international control, as well as to ensure that the resources released by effective disarmament measures are used for comprehensive development, in particular that of the developing countries.

Article - 8

1. States should undertake, at the national level, all necessary measures for the realization of the right to development and shall

ensure, inter alia, equality of opportunity for all in their access to basic resources, education, health services, food, housing, employment and the fair distribution of income. Effective measures should be undertaken to ensure that women have an active role in the development process. Appropriate economic and social reforms should be carried out with a view to eradicating all social injustices.

2. States should encourage popular participation in all spheres as an important factor in development and in the full realization of all human rights.

Article - 9

1. All the aspects of the right to development set forth in the present Declaration are indivisible and interdependent and each of them should be considered in the context of the whole.

2. Nothing in the present Declaration shall be construed as being contrary to the purposes and principles of the United Nations, or as implying that any State, group or person has a right to engage in any activity or to perform any act aimed at the violation of the rights set forth in the Universal Declaration of Human Rights and in the International Covenants of Human Rights.

Article - 10

Steps should be taken to ensure the full exercise and progressive enhancement of the right to development, including formulation, adopti‹ and implementation of policy, legislative land other measures at the national and international levels.

APPENDIX G

CONVENTION ON THE RIGHTS OF THE CHILD

Reproduced below are parts of this **Convention** which was adopted by the General Assembly of the United Nations on 20 November 1989 and came in force on 2 September 1990.

PREAMBLE

The States Parties to the present Convention

Considering that, in accordance with the principles proclaimed in the Charter of the United Nations, recognition of the inherent dignity and of the equal and inalienable, rights of all members of the human family is the foundation of freedom, justice and peace in the world.

Bearing in mind that the peoples of the United Nations have, in the Charter, reaffirmed their faith in fundamental human rights and in the dignity and worth of the human person, and have determined to promote social progress and better standards of life in larger freedom.

Recognizing that, the United Nations has, in the Universal Declaration of Human Rights and in the International Covenants on Human Rights, proclaimed and agreed that everyone is entitled to all the rights and freedoms set forth therein, without distinction of any kind, such as race, colour, sex, language, religion, political or other opinion, national or social origin, property, birth or other status.

Recalling that, in the Universal Declaration of Human Rights, the United Nations has proclaimed that childhood is entitled to special care and assistance,

Convinced that the family, as the fundamental group of society and the natural environment for the growth and well-being of all its members and particularly children, should be afforded the necessary protection and assistance so that it can fully assume its responsibilities within the community.

Recognizing that the child, for the full and harmonious development of his or her personality, should grow up in a family environment, in an atmosphere of happiness, love and understanding.

Considering that the child should be fully prepared to live an individual life in society, and brought up in the spirit of the ideals proclaimed in the Charter of the United Nations, and in particular in the spirit of peace, dignity, tolerance, freedom, equality and solidarity.

Bearing in mind that the need to extend particular care to the child has been stated in the Geneva Declaration of the Rights of the Child of 1924 and in the Declaration of the Rights of the Child adopted by the General Assembly on 20 November 1959 and recognized in the Universal Declaration of Human Rights, in the International Covenant on Civil and Political Rights (in particular in Articles 23. And 24), in the International Covenant on Economic, Social and Cultural Rights (in particular in Article 10) and in the statutes and relevant instruments of specialized agencies and international organizations concerned with the welfare of children.

Bearing in mind that, as indicated in the Declaration of the Rights of the Child, "the child, by reason of his physical and mental immaturity, needs special safeguards and care, including appropriate legal protection, before as well as after birth".

Recalling the provisions of the Declaration on Social and Legal Principles relating to the Protection and Welfare of Children, with Special Reference to Foster Placement and Adoption Nationally and internationally, the United Nations Standard Minimum Rules for the Administration of Juvenile Justice (The Beijing Rules); and the Declaration on the Protection of Women and Children in Emergency and Armed Conflict.

Recognizing that, in all countries in the world, there are children living in exceptionally difficult conditions, and that such children need special consideration.

Taking due account of the importance of the traditions and cultural values of each people for the protection and harmonious development of the child.

Recognizing the importance of International cooperation for improving the living conditions of children in every country, in particular in the developing countries.

Have agreed as follows:

PART - 1

Article - 1

For the purposes of the present Convention, a child means every human being below the age of eighteen years unless, under the law applicable to the child, majority is attained earlier.

Article - 2

1. States Parties shall respect and ensure the rights set forth in the present Convention to each child within their jurisdiction without discrimination of any kind irrespective of the child's or his or her parent's or legal guardian's race, colour, sex, language, religion, political or other opinion, national, ethnic or social origin, property, disability, birth or other status.

2. States Parties shall take all appropriate measures to ensure that the child is protected against all forms of discrimination or punishment on the basis of the status, activities, expressed opinions, or beliefs of the child's parents, legal guardians, or family members.

Article - 3

1. In all actions concerning children, whether undertaken by public or private social welfare institutions, courts of law, administrative authorities or legislative bodies, the best interests of the child shall be a primary consideration.

2. States Parties undertake to ensure the child such protection and care as is necessary for his or her wellbeing, taking into account the rights and duties of his or her parents, legal guardians, or other individuals legally responsible for him or her, and to this end, shall take all appropriate legislative and administrative measures.

Article - 5

States Parties shall respect the responsibilities, rights and duties of parents or, where applicable, the members of the extended family or community as provided for by local custom, legal guardians or other persons legally responsible for the child, to provide, in a manner consistent with the evolving capacities of the child, appropriate direction and guidance in the exercise by the child of the rights recognized in the present Convention.

Article - 6

1. States Parties recognize that every child has the inherent right to life.
2. States Parties shall ensure to the maximum extent possible the survival and development of the child.

Article - 7

1. The child shall be registered immediately after birth and shall have the right from birth to a name, the right to acquire a nationality and as far as possible, the right to know and be cared for by his or her parents.

*   *   *   *   *

Article - 9

1. States Parties shall ensure that a child shall not be separated from his or her parents against their will, except when competent authorities subject to judicial review determine, in accordance with applicable law and procedures, that such separation is necessary for the best interests of the child. Such determination may be necessary in a particular case such as one involving abuse or neglect of the child by the parents, or one where the parents are living separately and a decision must be made as to the child's place of residence.

*   *   *   *   *

Article - 11

1. States Parties shall take measures to combat the illicit transfer and non-return of children abroad.

2. To this end, States Parties shall promote the conclusion of bilateral or multilateral agreements or accession to existing agreements.

Article - 12

1. States Parties shall assure to the child who is capable of forming his or her own views the right to express those views freely in all matters affecting the child, the views of the child being given due weight in accordance with the age and maturity of the child.

Article - 13

1. The child shall have the right to freedom of expression; this right shall include freedom to seek, receive and impart information and ideas of all kinds, regardless of frontiers, either orally, in writing or in print, in the form of art, or through any other media of the child's choice.

Article - 14

1. States Parties shall respect the right of the child to freedom of thought, conscience and religion.

2. States Parties shall respect the rights and duties of the parents and when applicable legal guardians, to provide direction to the child in the exercise of his or her right in a manner consistent with the evolving capacities of the child.

3. Freedom to manifest one's religion or beliefs may be subject only to such limitations as are prescribed by law and are necessary to protect public safety, order, health or morals, or the fundamental rights and freedoms of others.

Article - 15

1. States Parties recognize the rights of the child to freedom of association and to freedom of peaceful assembly.

2. No restrictions may be placed on the exercise of these rights other than those imposed in conformity with the law and which are necessary in a democratic society in the interests of national security or public safety, public order (order public), the protection of public health or morals or the protection of the rights and freedoms of others.

Article - 16

1. No child shall be subjected to arbitrary or unlawful interference with his or her privacy, family, home or correspondence, nor to unlawful attacks on his or her honour and reputation.

2. The child has the right to the protection of the law against such interference or attacks.

Article - 17

States Parties recognize the important function performed by the mass media and shall ensure that the child has access to information and material from a diversity of national and international sources, especially those aimed at the promotion of his or her social, spiritual and moral well-being and physical and mental health. To this end, States Parties shall:

a. encourage the mass media to disseminate information and material of social and cultural benefit to the child and in accordance with the spirit of Article 29:

b. encourage international cooperation in the production, exchange and dissemination of such information and material from a diversity of cultural, national and international sources;

c. encourage the production and dissemination of children's books;

d. encourage the mass media to have particular regard to the linguistic needs of the child who belongs to a minority group or who is indigenous;

e. encourage the development of appropriate guidelines for the protection of the child from information and material injurious to his or her well-being, bearing in mind the provisions of Articles 13 and 18.

Article - 18

1. States Parties shall use their best efforts to ensure recognition of the principle that both parents have common responsibilities for the upbringing and development of the child. Parents or, as the case may be legal guardians, have the primary responsibility for the upbringing and development of the child. The best interests of the child will be their basic concern.

2. For the purpose of guaranteeing and promoting the rights set forth in the present Convention. States Parties shall render appropriate assistance to parents and legal guardians in the performance of their child-rearing responsibilities and shall ensure the development of institutions, facilities and services for the care of children.

3. States Parties shall take all appropriate measures to ensure that children of working parents have the right to benefit from child-care services and facilities for which they are eligible.

Article - 19

1. States Parties shall take all appropriate legislative, administrative, social and educational measures to protect the child from all forms of physical or mental violence, injury or abuse, neglect or negligent treatment, maltreatment or exploitation, including sexual abuse, while in the care of parent's, legal guardian's or any other person who has the care of the child.

Article - 20

1. A child temporarily or permanently deprived of his or her family environment, or in whose own best interest cannot be allowed to remain in that environment, shall be entitled to special protection and assistance provided by the State.

Article - 21

States Parties that recognize and/or permit the system of adoption shall ensure that the best interests of the child shall be the paramount consideration.

* * * * *

Article - 23

1. States Parties recognize that a mentally or physically disabled child should enjoy a full and decent life, in conditions which ensure dignity, promote self-reliance and facilitate the child's active participation in the community.

2. States Parties recognize the right of the disabled child to special care and shall encourage and ensure the extension, subject to available resources, to the eligible child and those responsible for

his or her care, of assistance for which application is made and which is appropriate to the child's condition and to the circumstances of the parents or others caring for the child.

3. Recognizing the special needs of a disabled child, assistance extended in accordance with paragraph 2 of the present Article shall be provided free of charge, whenever possible, taking into account the financial, resources of the parents or others caring for the child, and shall be designed to ensure that the disabled child has effective access to and receives education, training, health care services, rehabilitation services, preparation for employment and recreation opportunities in a manner conducive to the child's achieving the fullest possible social integration and individual development, including his or her cultural and spiritual development.

4. States Parties shall promote, in the spirit of international cooperation, the exchange of appropriate information in the field of preventive health care and of medical, psychological and functional treatment of disabled children, including dissemination of and access to information concerning methods of rehabilitation, education and vocational services, with the aim of enabling States Parties to improve their capabilities and skills and to widen their experience in these areas. In this regard, particular account shall be taken of the needs of developing countries.

Article - 24

1. States Parties recognize the right of the child to the enjoyment of the highest attainable standard of health and to facilities for the treatment of illness and rehabilitation of health. States Parties shall strive to ensure that no child is deprived of his or her right of access to such health care services.

2. States Parties shall pursue full implementation of this right and, in particular, shall take appropriate measures:

    a. to diminish infant and child mortality;

    b. to ensure the provision of necessary medical assistance and health care to all children with emphasis on the development of primary health care.

    c. to combat disease and malnutrition, including within the framework of primary health care, through, inter alia, application of readily available technology and through the provision of adequate nutritious foods and clean drinking-water, taking into consideration the dangers and risks of environment pollution;

d. to ensure appropriate pre-natal and post-natal health care for mothers;

e. to ensure that all segments of society, in particular parents and children, are informed, have access to education and are supported in the use of basic knowledge of child health and nutrition, the advantages of breast-feeding, hygiene and environmental sanitation and the prevention of accidents;

f. to develop preventive health care, guidance for parents and family planning education and services.

3. States Parties shall take all effective and appropriate measures with a view to abolishing traditional practices prejudicial to the health of children.

4. States Parties undertake to promote and encourage international cooperation with a view to achieving progressively the full realization of the right recognized in the present Article. In this regard, particular account shall be taken of the needs of developing countries.

Article - 27

1. States Parties recognize the right of every child to a standard of living adequate for the child's physical, mental, spiritual, moral and social development.

2. The parent's or others responsible for the child have the primary responsibility to secure, with their abilities and financial capacities, the conditions of living necessary for the child's development.

3. States parties, in accordance with national conditions and within their means, shall take appropriate measures to assist parents and others responsible for the child to implement this right and shall in case of need provide material assistance and support programmes, particularly with regard to nutrition, clothing and housing.

Article - 28

1. States Parties recognize the right of the child to education, and with a view to achieving this right progressively and on the basis of equal opportunity, they shall, in particular:
   a. make primary education compulsory and available free to all;
   b. encourage the development of different forms of secondary education, including general and vocational education, make them available and accessible to every child, and take appropriate measures such as the introduction of free education and offering financial assistance in case of need;
   c. make higher education accessible to all on the basis of capacity by every appropriate means;
   d. make educational and vocational information and guidance available land accessible to all children;
   e. take measures to encourage regular attendance at schools and the reduction of drop-out rates.
2. States Parties shall take all appropriate measures to ensure that school discipline is administered in a manner consistent with the child's human dignity and in conformity with the present Convention.
3. States Parties shall promote and encourage international cooperation in matters relating to education, in particular with a view to contributing to the elimination of ignorance and illiteracy throughout the world land facilitating access to scientific and technical knowledge and modern teaching methods. In this regard, particular account shall be taken of the needs of developing countries.

Article - 29

1. States Parties agree that the education of the child shall be directed to:
   a. the development of the child's personality, talents and mental and physical abilities to their fullest potential;
   b. the development of respect for human rights and fundamental freedoms, and for the principles enshrined in the Charter of the United Nations;

c. the development of respect for the child's parents, his or her own cultural identity, language and values, for the national values of the country in which the child is living, the country from which he or she may originate, and for civilizations different from his or her own;

d. the preparation of the child for responsible life in a free society, in the spirit of understanding, peace, tolerance, equality of sexes, and friendship among all peoples, ethnic, national and religious groups and persons of indigenous origin;

e. the development of respect for the natural environment.

2. No part of the present Article or Article 28 shall be construed so as to interfere with the liberty of individuals and bodies to establish and direct educational institutions, subject always to the observance of the principles set forth in paragraph 1 of the present Article and to the requirements that the education given in such institutions shall conform to such minimum standards as may be laid down by the State.

Article - 30

In those States in which ethnic, religious or linguistic minorities or persons of indigenous origin exist, a child belonging to such a minority or who is indigenous shall not be denied the right, in community with other members of his or her group, to enjoy his or her own culture, to profess and practise his or her own religion, or to use his or her own language.

Article - 31

1. States parties recognize the right of the child to rest and leisure, to engage in play and recreational activities appropriate to the age of the child and to participate freely in cultural life and the arts.

2. States Parties shall respect and promote the right of the child to participate fully in cultural and artistic life and shall encourage the provision of appropriate and equal opportunities for cultural, artistic, recreational and leisure activity.

Article - 32

1. States parties recognize the right of the child to be protected from economic exploitation and from performing any work that is likely to be hazardous or to interfere with the child's education, or to be harmful to the child's health or physical, mental, spiritual, moral or social development.

2. States Parties shall take legislative, administrative, social and educational measures to ensure the implementation of the present Article. To this end, and having regard to the relevant provisions of other international instruments. States Parties shall in particular;

   a. provide for a minimum age or minimum ages for admission to employment;

   b. provide for appropriate regulations of the hours and conditions of employment;

   c. provide for appropriate penalties or other sanctions to ensure the effective enforcement of the present Article.

Article - 33

States parties shall take all appropriate measures, including legislative, administrative, social and educational measures, to protect children from the illicit use of narcotic drugs and psychotropic substances as defined in the relevant international treaties, and to prevent the use of children in the illicit production and trafficking of such substances.

Article - 34

States Parties undertake to protect the child from all forms of sexual exploitation and sexual abuse. For these purposes, States Parties shall in particular take all appropriate national, bilateral and multilateral measures to prevent:

a. the inducement or coercion of a child to engage in any unlawful sexual activity;

b. the exploitative use of children in prostitution or other unlawful sexual practices;

c. the exploitative use of children in pornographic performances and materials.

Article - 35

States Parties shall take all appropriate national, bilateral and multilateral measures to prevent the abduction of, the sale of or traffic in children for any purpose or in any form.

Article - 36

States Parties shall protect the child against all other forms of exploitation prejudicial to any aspects of the child's welfare.

Article - 37

States Parties shall ensure that:

a. no child shall be subjected to torture or other cruel, inhuman or degrading treatment or punishment. Neither capital punishment nor life imprisonment without possibility of release shall be imposed for offences committed by persons below eighteen years of age;

b. no child shall be deprived of his or her liberty unlawfully or arbitrarily. The arrest, detention or imprisonment of a child shall be in conformity with the law and shall be used only as a measure of last resort and for the shortest appropriate period of time;

c. every child deprived of liberty shall be treated with humanity and respect for the inherent dignity of the human person, and in a manner which takes into account the needs of persons of his or her age. In particular, every child deprived of liberty shall be separated from adults unless it is considered in the child's best interest not to do so and shall have the right to maintain contact with his or her family through correspondence and visits, save in exceptional circumstances;

d. every child deprived of his or her liberty shall have the right to prompt access to legal and other appropriate assistance, as well as the right to challenge the legality of the deprivation of his or her liberty before a court or other competent, independent and impartial authority, and to a prompt decision on any such action.

Article - 38

1. States Parties undertake to respect and to ensure respect for rules of international humanitarian law applicable to them in armed conflicts which are relevant to the child.

2. States Parties shall take all feasible measures to ensure that persons who have not attained the age of fifteen years do not take a direct part in hostilities.

3. States Parties shall refrain from recruiting any person who has not attained the age of fifteen years into their armed forces.

4. In accordance with their obligations under international humanitarian law to protect the civilian population in armed conflicts, States Parties shall take all feasible measures to ensure protection and care of children who are affected by an armed conflict.

Article - 39

States Parties shall take all appropriate measures to promote physical and psychological recovery and social reintegration of a child victim of: any form of neglect exploitation, or abuse; torture or any other form of cruel, inhuman or degrading treatment or punishment; or armed conflicts. Such recovery and reintegration shall take place in an environment which fosters the health, self-respect and dignity of the child..

PART - 2

Article - 42

States Parties undertake to make the principles land provisions of the Convention widely known, by appropriate and active means, to adults and children alike.

APPENDIX H

THE VIENNA DECLARATION AND PROGRAMME OF ACTION

The World Conference on Human Rights was held at Vienna, Austria, from 14 to 25 June 1993. The Conference, the largest ever gathering of this kind was attended by about 7000 participants representing 171 States and numerous national and international bodies and non-government organizations. The objectives of the Conference were, among others, to 'review and assess progress made in the field of human rights since the adoption of the Universal Declaration of Human Rights in 1948, examine the link between development and the enjoyment of economic, social, cultural, civil and political rights, identify obstacles and ways in which they might be overcome'. Reproduced below are some parts of this Declaration.

Part - 1

1. The World Conference of Human Rights reaffirms the solemn commitment of all Sates to fulfill their obligations to promote universal respect for, and observance and protection of, all human rights and fundamental freedoms for all in accordance with the Charter of the United Nations, other instruments relating to human rights, and international law. The universal nature of these rights and freedoms is beyond question.

   In this framework, enhancement of international cooperation in the field of human rights is essential for the full achievement of the purposes of the United Nations.

   Human rights and fundamental freedoms are the birthright of all human beings; their protection and promotion is the first responsibility of Governments.

2. All peoples have the right of self-determination. By virtue of that right they freely determine their political status, and freely pursue their economic, social and cultural development.

Taking into account the particular situation of peoples under colonial or other forms of alien domination or foreign occupation, the World Conference on Human Rights recognize the right of peoples to take any legitimate action, in accordance with the Charter of the United Nations, to realize their inalienable right of self-determination. The World Conference on Human Rights considers the denial of the right of self-determination as a violation of human rights and underlines the importance of the effective realization of this right.

*   *   *   *   *

5. All human rights are universal, indivisible and interdependent and interrelated. The international community must treat human rights globally in a fair and equal manner, on the same footing, and with the same emphasis. While the significance of national and regional particularities and various historical, cultural and religious backgrounds must be borne in mind, it is the duty of States, regardless of their political, economic and cultural systems, to promote land protect all human rights and fundamental freedoms.

*   *   *   *   *

8. Democracy, development and respect for human rights and fundamental freedoms are interdependent and mutually reinforcing. Democracy is based on the freely expressed will of the people to determine their own political, economic, social and cultural systems and their full participation in all aspects of their lives. In the context of the above, the promotion and protection of human rights and fundamental freedoms at the national and international levels should be universal and conducted without conditions attached. The international community should support the strengthening and promoting of democracy, development and respect for human rights and fundamental freedoms in the entire world.

9. The World Conference of Human Rights reaffirms that least developed countries committed to the process of democratization and economic reforms, many of which are in Africa, should be supported by the international community in order to succeed in their transition to democracy and economic development.

10. The World Conference on Human Rights reaffirms the right to development, as established in the Declaration on the Right to

Development, as a universal and inalienable right and an integral part of fundamental human rights.

As stated in the declaration on the Right to Development, the human person is the central subject of development.

While development facilitates the enjoyment of all human rights, the lack of development may not be invoked to justify the abridgement of internationally recognized human rights.

States should cooperate with each other in ensuring development and eliminating obstacles to development. The international community should promote an effective international cooperation for the realization of the right to development and elimination of obstacles to development.

Lasting progress towards the implementation of the right to development requires effective development policies at the national level, as well as equitable economic relations and a favourable economic environment at the international level.

11. The right to development should be fulfilled so as to meet equitably the developmental and environmental needs of present and future generations. The World Conference on Human Rights recognizes that illicit dumping of toxic and dangerous substances and waste potentially constitutes a serious threat to the human rights to life and health of everyone.

Everyone has the right to enjoy the benefits of scientific progress and its applications. The World Conference on Human Rights notes that certain advances, notably in the biomedical and life sciences as well as in information technology, may have potentially adverse consequences for the integrity, dignity and human rights of the individual, and calls for international cooperation to ensure that human rights and dignity are fully respected in this area of universal concern.

12. The World Conference on Human Rights calls upon the international community to make all efforts to help alleviate the external debt burden of developing countries, in order to supplement the efforts of the Government of such countries to attain the full realization of the economic, social and cultural rights of their people.

* * * * *

14. The existence of widespread extreme poverty inhibits the full and effective enjoyment of human rights; its immediate alleviation and eventual elimination must remain a high priority for the international community.

15. Respect for human rights and for fundamental freedoms without distinction of any kind is a fundamental rule of international human rights law. The speedy and comprehensive elimination of all forms of racism and racial discrimination, xenophobia and related intolerance is a priority task for the international community. Governments should take effective measures to prevent and combat them.

16. The World Conference on Human Rights welcome the progress made in dismantling apartheid and calls upon the international community and the United Nations system to assist in this process.

17. The acts, methods and practices of terrorism in all its forms and manifestations as well as linkage in some countries to drug trafficking are activities aimed at the destruction of human rights, fundamental freedoms and democracy, threatening territorial integrity, security of States and destabilizing legitimately constituted Governments. The international community should take the necessary steps to enhance cooperation to prevent and combat terrorism.

18. The human rights of women and of the girl-child are an inalienable, integral and indivisible part of universal human rights. The full and equal participation of women in political, civil, economic, social and cultural life, at the national, regional and international levels, and the eradication of all forms of discrimination on grounds of sex are priority objectives of the international community.

Gender-based violence and all forms of sexual harassment and exploitation including those resulting from cultural prejudice and international trafficking, are incompatible with the dignity and worth of the human person, and must be eliminated.

19. Considering the importance of the promotion and protection of the rights of persons belonging to minorities and the contribution of such promotion and protection to the political and social stability of the States in which such persons live.

The World Conference on Human Rights reaffirms the obligation of States to ensure that persons belonging to minorities and the contribution of such promotion and protection to the political and social stability of the States in which such persons live.

The persons belonging to minorities have the right to enjoy their own culture, to profess and practise their own religion and to use their own language in private and in public, freely and without interference or any form of discrimination.

20. The World Conference on Human Rights recognizes the inherent dignity and the unique contribution of indigenous people to the development and plurality of society and strongly reaffirms the commitment of the international community to their economic, social and cultural well-being and their enjoyment of the fruits of sustainable development. States should ensure the full and free participation of indigenous people in all aspects of society, in particular in matters of concern to them. Considering the importance of the promotion and protection of the rights of indigenous people, and the contribution of such promotion and protection to the political and social stability of the states in which such people live. State should, in accordance with international law, take concerted positive steps to ensure respect for all human rights and fundamental freedoms of indigenous people, on the basis of equality and non-discrimination, and recognize the value and diversity of their distinct identities, cultures and social organization.

* * * * *

22. Special attention needs to be paid to ensuring non-discrimination, and the equal enjoyment of all human rights and fundamental freedoms by disabled persons, including their active participation in all aspects of society.

23. The World Conference on Human Rights reaffirms that everyone, without distinction of any kind, is entitled to the right to seek and to enjoy in other countries asylum from persecution, as well as the right to return to one's own country.

The World Conference on Human Rights recognizes that gross violation of human rights, including in armed conflicts, are among the multiple and complex factors leading to displacement of people.

The World Conference of Human Rights recognizes that, in view of the complexities of the global refugee crisis and in accordance with the Charter of the United Nations, relevant international instruments and international solidarity and in the spirit of burden-sharing, a comprehensive approach by the international community is needed in coordination and cooperation with the countries concerned and relevant organizations, bearing in mind the mandate of the United Nations High Commissioner for Refugees.

In accordance with the Charter of the United Nations and the principles of humanitarian law, the World Conference on Human Rights further emphasized the importance of and the need for humanitarian assistance to victims of all natural and man-made disasters.

24. Great importance must be given to the promotion and protection of the human rights of persons belonging to groups which have been rendered vulnerable, including migrant workers, the elimination of all forms of discrimination against them, and the strengthening and more effective implementation of existing human rights instruments.

25. The World Conference on Human Rights affirms that extreme poverty and social exclusion constitute a violation of human dignity and that urgent steps are necessary to achieve better knowledge of extreme poverty and its causes, including those related to the problem of development, in order to promote the human rights of the poorest, and to put an end to extreme poverty and social exclusion and to promote the enjoyment of the fruits of social progress. It is essential for States to foster participation by the poorest people in the decision-making process by the community in which they live, the promotion of human rights and efforts to combat extreme poverty.

* * * * *

28 The World Conference on Human Rights expresses its dismay at massive violations of human rights especially in the form of genocide, "ethnic cleansing" and systematic rape of women in war situations, creating mass exodus of refugees and displaced persons. While strongly condemning such abhorrent practices it reiterates the call that perpetrators of such crimes be punished and such practices immediately stopped.

29 The World Conference on Human Rights expresses grave concern about continuing human rights violations in all parts of the world in disregard of standards as contained in international human rights instruments and international humanitarian law and about the lack of sufficient and effective remedies for the victims.

30 The World Conference on Human Rights also expresses its dismay and condemnation that gross and systematic violations and situations that constitute serious obstacles to the full enjoyment of all human rights continue to occur in different parts of the world. Such violations and obstacles include, as well as torture and cruel, inhuman and degrading treatment or punishment, summary and arbitrary executions, disappearances, arbitrary detentions, all forms of racism, racial discrimination and apartheid, foreign occupation and alien domination, xenophobia, poverty, hunger and other denials of economic, social and cultural rights, religious intolerance, terrorism, discrimination against women and lack of the rule of law.

31 The World Conference on Human Rights calls upon States to refrain from any unilateral measure not in accordance with international law and the Charter of the United Nations that creates obstacles to trade relations among States and impedes in full realization of the human rights set forth in the Universal Declaration of Human Rights and international human rights instruments, in particular the rights of everyone to a standard of living adequate for their health and well-being, including food and medical care, housing and the necessary social services. The World Conference on Human Rights affirms that food should not be used as a tool for political pressure.

32 The World Conference on Human Rights reaffirms the importance of ensuring the university, objectivity and non-selectivity of the consideration of human rights issues.

33 The World Conference on Human Rights reaffirms that States are duty-bound, as stipulated in the Universal Declaration of Human Rights and the International Covenant on Economic, Social and Cultural Right and in other international human rights instruments, to ensure that education is aimed at strengthening the respect of human rights and fundamental freedoms. The World Conference on Human Rights emphasized the importance of incorporating

the subject of human rights education programmes and calls upon States to do so. Education should promote understanding, tolerance, peace and friendly relations between the nations and all racial or religious groups and encourage the development of United Nations activities in pursuance of these objectives. Therefore, education on human rights and the dissemination of proper information, both theoretical and practical, play and important role in the promotion and respect of human rights with regard to all individuals without distinction of any kind such as race, sex, language or religion, and this should be integrated in the education policies at the national as well as international levels. The World conference on Human Rights notes that resource constraints and institutional inadequacies may impede the immediate realization of these objectives.

36 The World Conference on Human Rights reaffirms the important and constructive role played by national institutions for the promotion and protection of human rights, in particular in their advisory capacity to the competent authorities, their role in remedying human rights violations, in the dissemination of human rights information, and education in human rights.

The World Conference on Human Rights encourages the establishment and strengthening of national institutions, having regard to the "Principles relating to the status of national institutions" and recognizing that it is the right of each State to choose the framework which is best suited to its particular needs at the national level.

PART - 2

B. Equality, Dignity and Tolerance

1. Racism, Racial Discrimination, Xenophobia and Other Forms of Intolerance

19. The World Conference on Human Rights considers the elimination of racism and racial discrimination, in particular in their institutionalized forms such as apartheid or resulting from doctrines of racial superiority or exclusivity or contemporary forms and manifestations of racism, as a primary objective for the international community and a world-wide promotion programme in the field of human rights.

21. The World Conference on Human Rights urges all Governments to take immediate measures and to develop strong policies to prevent and combat all forms and manifestations of racism, xenophobia or related intolerance, where necessary by enactment of appropriate legislation, including penal measures, and by the establishment of national institutions to combat such phenomena.

22. The World Conference on Human Rights calls upon all Governments to take all appropriate measures in compliance with their international obligations and with due regard to their respective legal systems to counter intolerance and related violence based on religions or belief, including practices of discrimination against women and including the desecration of relations sites, recognizing that every individual has the right to freedom of thought, conscience, expression and religion.

23. The World Conference on Human Rights stresses that all persons who perpetrate or authorize criminal acts associated with ethnic cleansing are individually responsible and accountable for such human rights violations, and that the international community should exert every effort to bring those legally responsible for such violations to justice.

24. The World Conference on Human Rights calls on all States to take immediate measures, individually and collectively, to combat the practice of ethnic cleansing to bring it quickly to an end. Victims of the abhorrent practice of ethnic cleansing are entitled to appropriate and effective remedies.

2. *Persons Belonging to National or Ethnic, Religious and Linguistic Minorities*

26. The World Conference on Human Rights urges States and the international community to promote and protect the rights of persons belonging to national or ethnic, religious and linguistic minorities in accordance with the Declaration on the Rights of Persons belonging to National or Ethnic, Religious and Linguistic Minorities.

27. Measures to be taken, where appropriate, should include facilitation of their full participation in all aspects of the political, economic, social, religious and cultural life of society and in the economic progress and development in their country.

* * * * *

31. The World Conference on Human Rights urges States to ensure the full and free participation of indigenous people in all aspects of society, in particular in matters of concern to them.

* * * * *

33. The World Conference on Human Rights urges all States to guarantee the protection of the human rights of all migrant workers and their families.

34. The World Conference on Human Rights considers that the creation of conditions to foster greater harmony and tolerance between migrant workers and the rest of the society of the State in which they reside is of particular importance.

4. *The Rights of the Child*

* * * * *

47. The World Conference on Human Rights urges all nations to undertake measures to the maximum extent of their available resources, with the support of international cooperation, to achieve the goals in the World Summit Plan of Action. The Conference calls on States to integrate the Convention on the Rights of the Child into their national action plans. By means of these national action plans and through international efforts, particular priority should be placed on reducing infant, and maternal mortality rates, reducing malnutrition and illiteracy rates and providing access to safe drinking water and the basic education. Whenever so called for, national plans of action should be devised to combat devastating emergencies resulting from natural disasters and armed conflicts and the equally grave problem of children in extreme poverty.

48. The World Conference on Human Rights urges all States, with the support of international cooperation, to address the acute problem of children under especially difficult circumstances. Exploitation and abuse of children should be actively combated, including by addressing their root causes. Effective measures are required against female infanticide, harmful child labour, sale of children and organs, child prostitution, child pornography, as well as other forms of sexual abuse.

49. The World Conference on Human Rights supports all measures by the United Nations and its specialized agencies to ensure the effective protection and promotion of human rights of the girl child. The World conference on Human Rights urges States to repeal existing laws and regulations and remove customs and practices which discriminate against and cause harm to the girl-child.

50. The World Conference on Human Rights strongly supports the proposal that the secretary-general initiate a study into means of improving the protection of children in armed conflicts. Humanitarian norms should be implemented and measures taken in order to protect and facilitate assistance to children in war zones. Measures should include protection for children against indiscriminate use of all weapons of war, especially antipersonnel mines. The need for aftercare and rehabilitation of children traumatized by war must be addressed urgently. The Conference calls on the Committee on the Rights of the Child to study the question of raising the minimum age of recruitment into armed forces.

* * * * *

5. *Freedom from Torture*

* * * * *

57. The World Conference on Human Rights therefore urges all States to put an immediate end to the practice of torture and eradicate this evil for ever through full implementation of the Universal Declaration of Human Rights as well as the relevant conventions and where necessary, strengthening of existing mechanisms.

62. The World Conference on Human Rights, welcoming the adoption by the General Assembly of the Declaration on the Protection of all Persons from Enforced disappearance, calls upon all States to take effective legislative, administrative, judicial or other measures to prevent, terminate and punish acts of enforced disappearances. The World Conference on Human Rights reaffirms that it is the duty of all States, under any circumstances, to make investigations whenever there is reason to believe that an enforced disappearance

has taken place on a territory under their jurisdiction and if allegations are confirmed, to prosecute its perpetrators.

6. The Rights of the Disabled Person

63. The World Conference on Human Rights reaffirms that all human rights and fundamental freedoms are universal and thus unreservedly include persons with disabilities. Every person is born equal and has the same rights to life and welfare, education and work, living independently and active participation in all aspects of society. Any direct discrimination or other negative discriminatory treatment of a disabled person is therefore a violation of his or her rights. The World conference on Human Rights calls on Governments, where necessary, to adopt or adjust legislation to assure access to these and other frights for disabled persons.

64. The place of disabled persons is everywhere. Persons with disabilities should be guaranteed equal opportunity through the elimination of all socially determined barriers, be they physical, financial, social or psychological, which exclude or restrict full participation in society.

* * * * *

D. Human Rights Education

78. The World Conference on Human Rights considers human rights education, training and public information essential for the promotion and achievement of stable and harmonious relations among communities and for fostering mutual understanding, tolerance and peace.

79. States should strive to eradicate illiteracy and should direct education towards the full development of the human personality and to the strengthening of respect for human rights and fundamental freedoms. The World Conference on Human Rights calls on all States and institutions to include human rights, humanitarian law, democracy and rule of law as subjects in the curricula of all learning institutions in formal and non-formal settings.

80. Human rights education should include peace, democracy, development and social justice, as set forth in international and

regional human rights instruments, in order to achieve common understanding and awareness with a view to strengthening universal commitment to human rights.

81. Taking into account the World Plan of Action on Education for Human Rights and Democracy, adopted in March 1993 by the International Congress on Education for Human Rights and Democracy of the United Nations Educational, Scientific and Cultural Organization, and other human rights instruments, the World Conference on Human Rights recommends that States develop specific programmes and strategies for ensuring the widest human rights education and the dissemination of public information, taking particular account of the human rights needs of women.

82. Governments, with the assistance of intergovernmental organizations, national institutions and non-governmental organizations, should promote an increased awareness of human rights and mutual tolerance. The World Conference on Human Rights underlines the importance of strengthening the World Public Information Campaign for Human Rights carried out by the United Nations. They should initiate and support education in human rights and undertake effective dissemination of public information in this field. The advisory services and technical assistance programmes of the United Nations system should be able to respond immediately to requests from States for educational and training activities in the field of human rights as well as for special education concerning standards as contained in international human rights instruments and in humanitarian law and their application to special groups such as military forces, law enforcement personnel, police and the health profession. The proclamation of a United Nations decadc for human rights education in order to promote, encourage and focus these educational activities should be considered.

APPENDIX I

UNIVERSAL DECLARATION OF HUMAN RIGHTS (UDHR) AND PROVISIONS OF INDIAN CONSTITUTION AND LAW

The framing of the **Constitution of India** had started about two years before the **Universal Declaration of Human Rights** was adopted. However, every Article of the Universal Declaration is reflected in the Indian Constitution, which was adopted by India's Constituent Assembly on 26 November 1949, and law. The following comparative chart shows the correspondence between different Articles of the Universal Declaration of Human Rights with the provisions of the Indian Constitution and law.

Comparative Chart Showing correspondence of Different Articles of Universal Declaration of Human Rights with the Provisions of Indian Constitution and Law

Sl.No. of Article	Declaration of Human Rights	Article No.	Provisions of the India Constitution and Law
1.	All men are born free land are equal in dignity and in their rights	14	The State shall not deny to any person equality before the law or the equal protection of the laws within the territory of India.
2	No discrimination on the ground of race, colour, sex, language, religion, and birth.	15	The State shall not discriminate against any citizen on grounds only of religion, race, caste, sex, place of birth of any of them.
3	Right of Life	21	No person shall be deprived of his life or personal liberty except according to procedure established by law.
4	No slavery	23	Traffic in human beings and *begar* and other forms of forced labour

(Contd...)

Sl.No. of Article	Declaration of Human Rights	Article No.	Provisions of the India Constitution and Law
			are prohibited and any contravention of this provision shall be an offence punishable in accordance with law.
5	No torture, cruelty, inhumanor degrading treatment	21	*State of Maharashtra vs. Ravikant S. Patil, (1991) 2 SCC 373. Handcuffing and parading of undertrial prisoner was held violative of rights under Article 21. *Bandhua Mukti Morcha vs. Union of India, (1984) 3 SCC 161 and (1991) 4 SCC 177, Right to live with human dignity held to be enshrined in Article 21. *Maneka Gandhi, vs Union of India (1978) 1 SCC 248. The expression "personal liberty" under Art. 21 is a phrase of wide amplitude and covers a variety of rights which go to constitute personal liberty of man including right to safety of his person.
6	Right to recognition everywhere as a person before the law.	14 & 21	
7	Equality before law	14	
8	Right to effective remedy	32	1. The right to move the Supreme Court by appropriate proceedings for the enforcement of the rights conferred by Part III of the Constitution is guaranteed. 2. Supreme Court shall issue directions or orders or writs, including writs in the nature of *habeas corpus*, *mandamus*, *prohibition*, *quo warranto* and *certiorari* whichever may be

*These are reference to the judgements of the Supreme Court of India.

(Contd...)

Sl.No. of Article	Declaration of Human Rights	Article No.	Provisions of the India Constitution and Law
			appropriate, for the enforcement of any of the rights conferred by this part. 3. The right guaranteed by this article shall not be suspended except as otherwise provided by this Constitution.
		226	Notwithstanding anything in Article 32, every High Court shall have power, throughout the territories in relation to which it exercises jurisdiction, to issue to any person or authority, including in appropriate cases, any Government, within those territories directions, orders or writs, including writs in the nature of habeas corpus, mandamus, prohibition, quo warranto and certiorari, or any of them, for the enforcement of any of the rights conferred by Part III and for any other purpose.
9	Arbitrary arrest and detention	22	1. No person who is arrested shall be detained in custody without being informed, as soon as may be, of the grounds for such arrest nor shall he be denied the right to consult, and to be defended by, a legal practitioner of his choice. 2. Every person who is arrested and detained in custody shall be produced before the nearest magistrate within a period of twenty-four hours of such arrest excluding the time necessary for the journey from the place of arrest to the court of the magistrate and no such person shall be detained in custody beyond the said period without the authority of a magistrate.

(Contd...)

Sl.No. of Article	Declaration of Human Rights	Article No.	Provisions of the India Constitution and Law
10	Public hearing and fair trial	39A	The State shall secure that the operation of the legal system promotes justice, on a basis of equal opportunity, and shall, in particular, provide free legal aid, by suitable legislation or schemes or any other way, to ensure that opportunities for securing justice are not denied to any citizen by reason of economic or other disabilities.
		304* (CCP)	Where in a trial before the Court, the accused is not represented by a pleader, and where it appears to the Court that the accused has not sufficient means to engage a pleader, the Court shall assign a pleader for his defence at the expense of the State.
		303* (CCP)	Any person accused of an offence before a Criminal Court, or against whom proceedings are instituted under this code, may of right be defended by a pleader of his choice.
		327* (CCP)	The place in which any Criminal Court is held for the purpose of inquiring into or trying any offence shall be deemed to be an open Court, to which the public generally may have access, so far as the same can conveniently contain them.
11	Presumption of innocence and Criminal Law until proved guilty in public trial. No retrospective declaration of offence nor retrospective		The Principle of Common Law, the Doctrine of Rule of Law, Presumption of Innocence till guilt is established.

*These provisions are from the Code of Criminal Procedure, 1973.

(Contd...)

Sl.No. of Article	Declaration of Human Rights	Article No.	Provisions of the India Constitution and Law
	objective of higher sentence by retrospective amendments		
		20	i) No person shall be convicted of any offence except for violation of the law in force at the time of the commission of the act charged as an offence. Nor be subjected to a penalty greater than that might have been inflicted under the law in force at the time of the commission of the offence.
12	Privacy, family, home, correspondence, reputation, protection of law against interference or of force		Each one is covered by the law enacted by parliament and is protected.
13	i) Freedom of Movement and Residence ii) Right to live and return to country	19	d. To move freely throughout the territory of India. e. To reside and settle in any part of the territory of India.
14	Right to Religion	25	All persons are equally entitled to freedom of conscience and free profession, practice and propagation of religion.
15	i) Right to Nationality ii) Change of Nationality	5	At the commencement of this Constitution, every person who has his domicile in the territory of India and (a) who was born in the territory of India; (b) either of whose parents was born in the territory of India; or (c) who has been ordinarily resident in the territory of India for not less than five years immediately preceding such commencement, shall be al citizen of India.
		9	No person shall be a citizen of India by virtue of Article 5 or be deemed to be a citizen of India by

(Contd...)

Sl.No. of Article	Declaration of Human Rights	Article No.	Provisions of the India Constitution and Law
			virtue of Article 6 or Article 8, if he has voluntarily acquired the citizenship of any foreign state.
		10	Every person who is or is deemed to be a citizen of India under any of the foregoing provisions of this Part shall, subject to the provisions of any law that may be made by Parliament, continue to be such citizen.
16	Marriage and Family		Covered by suitable legislation applicable to people of different religions
17	Property	300A	Persons not be deprived of property save by authority of law
18	Freedom of thought and conscience	25(I)	All persons are equally entitled to freedom of conscience and the right freely to profess, practise and propagate religion
19	Freedom of information and expression	19(a)	All citizens shall have the right to speech and expression
20	Peaceful assembly and association	19(b)	All citizens shall have the right to assemble peaceably and without arms
21	(i) Democracy	19(c)	To form associations or unions
		325	There shall be one general electoral roll for every territorial constituency for election to either House of Parliament or to the House or either House of the Legislature of a State and no person shall be ineligible for inclusion in any such roll or claim to be included in any special electoral roll for any such constituency on grounds only of religion, race, caste, sex or any of them.

(Contd...)

Sl.No. of Article	Declaration of Human Rights	Article No.	Provisions of the India Constitution and Law
		326	The elections to the House of the People and the Legislative Assembly of every State shall be on the basis of adult suffrage; that is to say, every person who is a citizen of India and who is not less than 18 years of age on such date as may be fixed in that behalf by or under any law made by the appropriate Legislature and is not otherwise disqualified under this Constitution or any law made by the appropriate Legislature on the ground of non-residence, unsoundness of mind, crime or corrupt or illegal practice, shall be entitled to be registered as a voter at any such election.
	(ii) Public Service	16(1)	There shall be equality of opportunity for all citizens in matters relating to employment or appointment to any office under the State.
		16(2)	No citizen shall, on grounds only of religion, race, caste, sex, descent, place of birth., residence or any of them, be ineligible for, or discriminated against in respect of, any employment or office under the State.
	(iii)	326	Elections
22	Social Security	38(I)	The state shall strive to promote the welfare of the people by securing and protecting as effectively as it may a social order in which justice, social, economic and political, shall inform all the institutions of the national life

(Contd...)

Sl.No. of Article	Declaration of Human Rights	Article No.	Provisions of the India Constitution and Law
23	(i) Right to work	41	The State shall, within the limits of its economic, capacity and development, make effective provision for securing the right to work, to education and to public assistance in cases of unemployment, old age, sickness and disablement, and in other cases of undeserved want.
	(ii) Right to equal pay	39(a)	The State shall, in particular, direct its policy towards securing - that the citizens, men and women equally, have the right to an adequate means of livelihood.
	(iii) Remuneration keeping human dignity	43	The State shall endeavour to secure, by suitable legislation or economic organization or in any other way, to all workers, agricultural, industrial or otherwise, work, a living wage, conditions of work ensuring a decent standard of life and full employment of leisure and social and cultural opportunities and in particular, the State shall endeavour to promote cottage industries on an individual or cooperative basis in rural areas.
	(iv) Right to form and join unions	19(I)c	
24	Right to rest, reasonable working hours	43	
25	(i) Standard of living adequate for health and well-being	47	The State shall regard the raising of the level of nutrition and the standard of living of its people and the improvement of public health as among its primary duties and in particular, the State shall endeavour to bring about prohibition of the consumption

(Contd...)

Sl.No. of Article	Declaration of Human Rights	Article No.	Provisions of the India Constitution and Law
			except for medicinal purposes of intoxicating drinks and of drugs which are injurious to health.
	(ii) Motherhood and Childhood	39(f)	The State shall in particular, direct its policy towards securing - that children are given opportunities and facilities to develop in a healthy manner and in conditions of freedom and dignity and that childhood and youth are protected against exploitation and against moral and material abandonment.
		42	The State shall make provision for securing just and humane conditions of work and for maternity relief.
26	Right to Education	45	The State shall endeavour to provide, within a period of ten years from the commencement of this Constitution, for free compulsory education for all children until they complete the age of fourteen years.
27	(i) Free participation in cultural life (ii) protection of moral and material interest	51(A)F	To value and preserve the rich heritage of our composite culture.
28	Social and international order	38	
		51	The State shall endeavour to (a) promote international peace and security; (b) maintain just and honourable relations (c) foster respect for international law and treaty obligations in the dealings of organized people with one another; and (d) encourage settlement of international disputes by arbitration.

(Contd. .)

Sl.No. of Article	Declaration of Human Rights	Article No.	Provisions of the India Constitution and Law
29	Duties	51A	It shall be the duty of every citizen of India - (a) to abide by the Constitution and respect its ideals and insitutions, the National Flag and the National anthem; (b) to cherish and follow the noble ideals which inspired our national struggle for freedom; (c) to uphold and protect the sovereignty, unity and integrity of India; (d) to defend the country and render national service when called upon to do so (e) to promote harmony and the spirit of common brotherhood amongst all the people of India transcending religious, linguistic and regional or sectional diversities; to renounce practices derogatory to the dignity of women; (f) to value and preserve the rich heritage of our composite culture; (g) to protect and improve the national environment including forests, lakes, rivers and wild life, and to have compassion for living creatures (h0 to develop the scientific temper, humanism and the spirit of inquiry and reform (i) to safeguard public property and to abjure violence and (j) to strive towards excellence in all spheres of individual and collective activity so that the nation constantly rises to higher levels of endeavour and achievement.

APPENDIX J

INDIAN LAWS RELATING TO HUMAN RIGHTS

The following is a list of some of the important national statutes which have a bearing on the promotion/protection of Human Rights.

1. Constitution of India (Preamble Parts III, IV and IVA, articles 226, 300A, 325, 326)

2. Protection of Human Rights Act, 1993.

   'The Act provides for the constitution of a National Human Rights Commission, State Human Rights Commissions, and Human Rights Courts for better protection of human rights'.

3. National Commission for Scheduled Castes and Scheduled Tribes.

   'Article 338 of the Constitution requires constitution of the National commission for Scheduled Castes and Scheduled Tribes for better protection of the rights of the members of the Scheduled Castes and Scheduled Tribes'.

4. National Commission for Minorities Act, 1992.

   'An Act to constitute a National Commission for Minorities for better protection of the rights of the minorities'.

5. National Commission for Women Act, 1990.

   'An Act to constitute a National Commission for Women for better protection of the rights of women'.

6. Protection of Civil Rights Act, 1955.

   'Under Article 17 of the Constitution, untouchability is abolished and its practice in any form is forbidden. By this Act, enforcement of any disability arising out of untouchability has been made an offence punishable in accordance with the relevant provisions'.

7. Scheduled Castes and Scheduled Tribes (Prevention of Atrocities) Act, 1989.

'An Act to prevent the commission of atrocities against the members of the Scheduled Castes and the Scheduled Tribes, for constitution of special courts for trial of such offences, and to provide relief and rehabilitation to the victims'.

8. Employment of Manual Scavengers and Construction of Dry Latrines (Prohibition) Act, 1993.

   'Fraternity, assuring the dignity of the individual is one of the objects proclaimed in the Preamble to the Constitution. Article 47 requires the State to raise the standard of living and improve the health of the people. This Act has been enacted to achieve goes objectives. It provides for the prohibition of all manual scavengers as well as construction or continuance of dry latrines and for the regulation of construction and maintenance of water-seal latrines'.

9. Immoral Traffic (Prevention) Act, 1956.

   'Article 23 of the Constitution prohibits traffic in human beings. On I May 1950, India ratified the International Convention for Suppression of Immoral Traffic in Women and Girls. This is an Act to give effect to the same'.

10. Indecent Representation of Women (Prohibition) Act, 1986.

    'An Act to prohibit indecent representation of women through advertisements or in publications, writings, paintings, figures, or in any other manner'.

11. Dowry Prohibition Act, 1961.

    'This is an Act to prohibit the evil practice of giving and taking of dowry'.

12. Commission of Sati (Prevention) Act, 1987.

    'Sati or burning or burying alive of widows or women is revolting to the feelings of human nature and is nowhere enjoined by any of the religions of India as an imperative duty. This is an Act for effective prevention of the commission of Sati and its glorification'.

13. Maternity Benefit Act, 1961.

    'This is an Act to provide maternity benefits, etc., and to regulate employment of women in certain establishments for certain periods before and after child birth'.

14. Child Marriage Restraint Act, 1929.

    'This was enacted with a view to preventing child marriages, namely, a marriage to which either of the contracting parties is under the specified age'.

15. Children (Pledging of Labour) Act, 1933.

    'An Act to prohibit the pledging of the labour of children and the employment of children whose labour has been pledged'.

16. Orphanages and Other Charitable Homes (Supervision and Control) Act, 1960.

    'An Act to provide for the supervision and control of orphanages, homes for neglected women or children and other like institutions and to penalize criminal activities indulged in such institutions'.

17. Children Act, 1960.

    'An Act to provide for the care, protection, maintenance, welfare, training, education and rehabilitation of children and for trial of delinquent children in the Union territories'.

18. Child Labour (Prohibition and Regulation) Act, 1986.

    'The Act bans employment of children in specified occupations and processes, lays down a procedure for inclusion in the schedule of banned occupations and processes and regulates the conditions of work of children in employment where they are not prohibited from working'.

19. Juvenile Justice Act, 1986.

    'An act to provide for the care, protection treatment, development and rehabilitation of neglected or delinquent juveniles and to provide a specialized approach for the juvenile justice system'.

20. Young Persons (Harmful Publications) Act, 1956.

    'Pictorial and other publications containing stories of crime, violence, cruelty or incidents of repulsive or horrible nature would tend to corrupt a young person and incite or encourage him to commit such acts. The Act seeks to prevent the dissemination of publications which are harmful to young persons'.

21. Caste Disabilities Removal Act, 1950.

'The Act provides that when in a civil suit the parties belong to different persuations, the laws of the religions of the parties shall not be permitted to operate to deprive such parties of any property to which but for the operation of such laws, they would have been entitled'.

22. Mental Health Act, 1987.

'The Act regulates determination of lunacy, reception, care and treatment of mentally ill persons'.

23. Bonded Labour (System) Abolition Act, 1976.

'Article 23 of the Constitution prohibits "begar" and other similar forms of forced labour and further provides that any contravention of the said prohibition shall be an offence punishable in accordance with law. That Act provides for the abolition of bonded labour system to prevent the economic and physical exploitation of the weaker sections of the people'.

Some other important statutes are the following:

1. The Pre-natal Diagnostic Techniques (Regulation and Prevention of Misuse) Act, 1994.
2. Medical Termination of Pregnancy Act, 1971.
3. The Transplantation of Human Organs Act, 1994.
4. Orphanages and Other Charitable Home (Supervision and Control) Act, 1960.
5. The SAARC Convention (Suppression of Terrorism) Act, 1993.
6. Environmental Protection Act, 1986.
7. Beedi and Cigar Workers (Conditions of Employment) act, 1966.
8. Beedi Workers Welfare Fund Act, 1976.
9. Trade Unions Act, 1926.
10. Industrial Disputes Act, 1947.
11. Workmen's Compensation Act, 1923.
12. Industrial Employment Standing Order Act, 1946.

13. Factories Act, 1948.
14. Employees State Insurance Act, 1948.
15. Minimum Wages Act, 1948.
16. The Employees Provident Funds and Miscellaneous Provisions Act, 1952.
17. Apprentices Act, 1961.
18. Equal Remuneration Act, 1976.
19. Payment of Wages Act, 1936.
20. Weekly Holidays Act, 1942.

INDEX